Praise for How to Start Your Own Business for Entrepreneurs

'At a time when more people than ever are starting a business, this second edition of an already very popular book is perfectly timed. Robert Ashton spells out what you need to do, step by step, to be a successful entrepreneur. What is unique is the way his book reassures and encourages even the most diffident business starter. This book makes it seem possible.'

DAWN WHITELEY, CEO, NATIONAL ENTERPRISE NETWORK,
www.nationalenterprisenetwork.org

'Full of practical advice interspersed with real-life case studies, How to Start your Own Business is an exhaustive resource for entrepreneurs embarking on an exhausting yet most exhilarating of journeys!'

ALAN GLEESON, GENERAL MANAGER, PALO ALTO
SOFTWARE & LIVEPLAN.COM

'I was introduced to Robert's writing by my customers. They said it was the best start-up book out there and I'm inclined to agree. This second edition is even better. Robert's updated it throughout and brought it bang up to date. There are now more than 50 real-life case studies, one of whom even mentions us! If you're starting a business you need two things to succeed. My software and Robert's book!'

DUANE JACKSON, FOUNDER AND MD, KASHFLOW ACCOUNTING
SOFTWARE, www.kashflow.com

'I'm something of a fan of Robert Ashton's books. He says it like it is using words that anyone can understand, even those of us that didn't go to college. This one is his best so far. It's a fantastic read and tells you all you need to know to start a business. Buy it, read it then do it!'

GARRY LEWIS, MD, YOUR ONE CALL LTD,

D1468869

PEARSON

At Pearson, we believe in learning – all kinds of learning for all kinds of people. Whether it's at home, in the classroom or in the workplace, learning is the key to improving our life chances.

That's why we're working with leading authors to bring you the latest thinking and the best practices, so you can get better at the things that are important to you. You can learn on the page or on the move, and with content that's always crafted to help you understand quickly and apply what you've learned.

If you want to upgrade your personal skills or accelerate your career, become a more effective leader or more powerful communicator, discover new opportunities or simply find more inspiration, we can help you make progress in your work and life.

Pearson is the world's leading learning company. Our portfolio includes the Financial Times, Penguin, Dorling Kindersley and our educational business, Pearson International.

Every day our work helps learning flourish, and wherever learning flourishes, so do people.

To learn more please visit us at: www.pearson.com/uk

How to Start Your Own Business

For Entrepreneurs

2nd Edition

Robert Ashton

PEARSON

Harlow, England • London • New York • Boston • San Francisco • Toronto • Sydney • Auckland • Singapore • Hong Kong
Tokyo • Seoul • Taipei • New Delhi • Cape Town • São Paulo • Mexico City • Madrid • Amsterdam • Munich • Paris • Milan

PEARSON EDUCATION LIMITED

Edinburgh Gate
Harlow CM20 2JE
Tel: +44 (0)1279 623623
Fax: +44 (0)1279 431059
Website: www.pearson.com/uk

First published in Great Britain in 2009
Second edition published 2012

© Pearson Education Limited 2009, 2012

Pearson Education is not responsible for the content of third-party internet sites.

ISBN: 978-0-273-77217-0

British Library Cataloguing-in-Publication Data
A catalogue record for this book is available from the British Library

Library of Congress Cataloging-in-Publication Data
Ashton, Robert, 1955-
  How to start your own business for entrepreneurs / Robert Ashton. -- 2nd ed.
    p. cm.
  ISBN 978-0-273-77217-0 (pbk.)
  1. New business enterprises. 2. Entrepreneurship. 3. Small business--Management.
I. Title.
  HD62.5.A817 2012
  658.1'1--dc23
                              2012010980

10 9 8 7 6 5 4 3 2 1
16 15 14 13 12

Text design by Design Deluxe
All cartoons © Jurgen Wolff
Typeset in 9/13pt Helvetica 45 Light by 30
Printed and bound in Great Britain by Ashford Colour Press Ltd, Gosport

Contents

About the author vii

Introduction to the second edition viii

Introduction to the first edition viii

How to use this book ix

Part One Before you start

1   See your future as an entrepreneur – crystal clear 3

2   How to find your biggest business opportunity 17

3   How to be really sure your business idea will fly 29

4   Business type – what's possible 41

5   Business structure – building in room to grow 51

6   Finding the perfect place – business premises 65

7   Starting up or taking over an existing enterprise 77

Part Two Planning to succeed

8   How to write a convincing plan 93

9   Where to find the money you need 103

10 Advisers and mentors and why they're important 117

11 Timing is everything – how to decide when to start 129

Part Three Finding customers

12 Where to look for the best customers 141

13 How to develop the right brand and image 151

14 Marketing in a nutshell 163

15 Your winning marketing message 175

16 How to make sure your website is a winner 185

17 How to get good PR and keep on getting it 197

18 Ways that anyone can be good at selling 211

19 Reputation – making friends and influencing people 223

Part Four *Managing your business*

20 How to do your bookkeeping without tears 235

21 How to make your profits bigger 245

22 Financial factors to watch as you start to grow 257

23 How to minimise risk and sleep well at night 269

24 Your first employee – how to take this giant leap 279

Part Five *Growing your business*

25 Measuring what matters 295

26 Lifestyle or wealth – a chance to reflect and review your goals 307

Index 324

About the author

Robert Ashton has started and sold three small businesses. He is passionate about how starting an enterprise enables people to take control of their future and create the lives they want for themselves.

A popular business speaker, Robert helps people discover the entrepreneur within themselves. He inspires, encourages and nurtures enterprise in all those with whom he works. He is in demand as a consultant, helping schools, charities and social enterprises, as well as business starters, achieve economic self-sufficiency and more.

How to Start Your Own Business for Entrepreneurs is a second edition. That means it's an improved, updated and completely refreshed version of an already best-selling book.

Find out more about Robert: **www.robertashton.co.uk**
Follow Robert on Twitter: **@robertashton1**

Introduction to the second edition

For an author to be invited to write a second edition is a rare privilege. Few business books enjoy lasting popularity and only one or two have ever become timeless classics. That's because times, attitudes and the ways we do business are constantly changing. This book sold very well in its original form, but the time had come to refresh it.

The original introduction, below, compares starting and growing a business to conceiving and raising a child. That metaphor remains strong for me and cannot be improved upon.

However, a second edition is like a second child. The basic structure of the book and the advice and tips it provides are the same, but the context and detail are very different. The economic climate has changed and the internet now plays a far bigger role in the way we do business.

It's also true to say that, as with a second child, I have seen new opportunities with this book. I think you'll find it easy to understand and the challenges it sets you readily achievable. Starting a business, like deciding to have a baby, is a very personal thing to do. It should also be pleasurable, and not a struggle.

I hope you enjoy this book and use it to create the future you want for yourself and those you love.

Introduction to the first edition

There is something magical about the birth of a new business. It's very like becoming a parent. The sense of awe and wonder that you have created something new will amaze you. If you're already a parent, you'll know what I mean.

Like a baby, your new business will need your constant care and attention. It will be completely dependent on you for its welfare and safety. Oblivious to danger, your new venture will need a healthy supply of cash, either from investment or customers. This book will show you what to do.

As your business grows, its demands on you will change. In fact, like a growing child, it will steadily develop and mature. Eventually, if you have reared it well, your business will become self-sufficient – able perhaps to support you now without your day-to-day involvement.

Creating your own enterprise presents a wider range of options than starting a family. Just as all babies have very similar needs so, too, do businesses. The difference is that not all businesses are the same. You might be planning to build a global empire or just develop an interest into a part-time business that fits around your other commitments. Although the basics will be the same, the scale and detail will be very different.

Businesses also grow at different rates. A part-time enterprise can take years to develop, while a company established to exploit a particular opportunity or piece of new technology might, of necessity, grow very fast.

It doesn't matter what your entrepreneurial aspirations are – this book will help you to make your business journey. Use it to nurture the seed of your business idea. Use the tips it contains to grow your enterprise and, importantly, learn from the experience of those who have already made the journey.

How to use this book

The way you use this book should be dictated by why you are reading it. If, for example, you hadn't planned to start a business, but changing circumstances have put self-employment high on your agenda, you'll probably start at the beginning and work through to the end.

If, however, you have already made plans and perhaps some progress, you'll be more likely to dip in and out of the book. But even if you already know much of what you need to know, there will be knowledge gaps these pages can usefully fill.

The text follows a logical sequence and the chapters are intentionally arranged so that the complete novice follows the best route. For example, you only need to worry about 'business structure' (Chapter Five) when you've worked out if your 'business idea will fly' in Chapter

Three. After all, only when you know the potential can you decide the best format.

If, like me, you like to scan a book and pick out the bits that catch your eye, you'll like the 'top tips'. These tell you the things I most want to share. They may also prompt you to dig deeper into the text in places.

There are also plenty of case studies. These illustrate the points each chapter makes, showing you how others have dealt with each of the key issues or opportunities.

Finally, because so many folk now are starting a business as a lifestyle choice, rather than because they aspire to make a million, you'll find high-lighted boxes throughout labelled 'lifestyle/high growth'. These will pick out for you some of the things you might do differently if you are building a lifestyle business or one you can quickly grow and perhaps sell.

As with so many aspects of enterprise, there is no right or wrong level of aspiration. Your business has to deliver the income you need and the opportunity for satisfaction and self-actualisation you want. The 'lifestyle/high growth' boxes will help you decide which is for you, at every step of the way.

Now it's time to start your journey through the book. Enjoy!

Before you start

Part One

See your future as an entrepreneur – crystal clear

Chapter One

You've decided to start your own business. You have a dream and want to turn it into reality. Inevitably your business vision will not yet be crystal clear. There will be doubts, concerns and many questions. Don't worry, that's normal. Let's work together on your concerns, answer your questions and help you gain an insight into your future as an entrepreneur.

How do entrepreneurs see the world?

To the experienced entrepreneur, the world is full of opportunities and interesting challenges. The opportunities are there to be evaluated and perhaps exploited. The challenges are merely obstacles to be overcome. Entrepreneurs have attitude!

The seasoned entrepreneur also appreciates that pitfalls are inevitable and success is always achieved at a price. The skills an entrepreneur develops over time enable them to:

→ see the opportunities that others may miss;
→ remain rational under pressure;
→ make objective, thought-through decisions;
→ never take setbacks personally.

Small opportunities are often the beginning of great enterprises. DEMOSTHENES

Mona's attempt to see her future as an entrepreneur was not entirely positive.

"You will meet a tall, dark stranger. He will be from the Inland Revenue."

How to Start Your Own Business for Entrepreneurs

Over time you, too, will acquire these skills. This book will help you until you do.

Case study

Daniel Koseoglu, The Tiffin Company
www.sheffield-catering.co.uk

Daniel left school with A levels and enjoyed a rapid rise up the corporate career ladder. His ability to improve operational efficiency, reducing costs without compromising safety, was quickly recognised. He worked for Royal Mail managing fuel supply operations, and Shell handling various maintenance contracts.

But corporate life did not give Daniel the sense of self-sufficiency or control he knew was achievable. His Turkish father ran a successful restaurant and had always been self-employed. Daniel decided to start his own business, turning his back on the relative security of corporate life.

Starting The Tiffin Company enabled Daniel to combine two quite different elements of his experience. He'd grown up with the food business, and logistics and operational management was what he'd excelled at since leaving school.

His company delivers pre-ordered lunches and event catering in traditional Asian reusable tiffin tins. The food is good, too, and the company is growing in popularity. Daniel is an entrepreneur. He took a calculated risk and now has a successful business. He's also keen to help other business starters succeed and has set up a young entrepreneur group in Sheffield.

How entrepreneurial are you?

The good news is that you are probably already entrepreneurial. Why else would you be planning to start a business? The challenge is to work out exactly how entrepreneurial you are. Or, to put it another way, how can you structure your ambition and your enterprise to best suit your personality and style?

We are all different, and it's important from the outset that your business gives you every opportunity to focus your efforts on what you do best. Equally, you need to appreciate what you might find less comfortable and make sure you don't create a business you won't actually enjoy.

Here are some questions to ask yourself. There are no right or wrong answers; nor are they questions that demand a yes/no answer. We need to work out where your greatest entrepreneurial strengths lie.

How competitive are you?

Some people just have to win at every opportunity. Others are simply content to take part. The more competitive you are, the more likely it is you will welcome the cut and thrust of business life. If, however, you are not competitive, you will probably have decided to start a business where it's less important to do marketplace battle with rivals.

COMPETITIVE PEOPLE

Are usually good at:	May not be too good at:
goal setting	attention to detail
selling	listening
self-motivation	losing

Remember that there is a lot more to business than being competitive. Your business does not have to be the best, just good enough.

How intuitive are you?

Intuitive entrepreneurs can sense what has to be done and when. They are usually pretty good at reading their marketplace and, in particular, at understanding exactly what their customers are expecting of them. If intuition is not one of your strengths you may need to work harder to measure what your customers are feeling about you.

INTUITIVE PEOPLE

Are usually good at:	May not be too good at:
reading a situation	believing market research
picking up good and bad vibes	asking obvious questions
trusting and following their instinct	justifying their actions

The more intuitive you are, the more likely you are to try things that have not been tried before.

How sensitive are you?

One of the first lessons you will learn as your business becomes established is not to take criticism personally. It is possible for somebody to have the highest regard for you and absolutely no interest in your business. Equally, you need to be tough enough to take rejection. Any business that wins every deal is not trying hard enough!

SENSITIVE PEOPLE

Are usually good at:	May not be too good at:
responding to feedback	accepting criticism
motivating people	giving negative feedback
adapting	sticking to their guns

How determined are you?

Determined people don't give up. They keep on trying after others have walked away. Sometimes determination is enough to win through although, on its own, it is rarely enough. People who lack determination often accept the status quo and will find easy routes to success.

DETERMINED PEOPLE

Are usually good at:	May not be too good at:
finding ways to overcome adversity	taking no for an answer
championing their business	bending to meet customer needs
remembering to do things	knowing when it's time to move on

How economical are you?

It's always good to be careful with money. Starting and growing a business presents countless opportunities to invest in the useful things.

The economical entrepreneur will spend frugally, buying only the things they really need. Someone more used to spending their money as fast as they earn it will find it harder to be economical.

ECONOMICAL PEOPLE

Are usually good at:	May not be too good at:
borrowing things	making investment decisions
buying well	encouraging customers to buy more
avoiding waste	maintaining quality

As a new entrepreneur you will be competitive, intuitive, sensitive, determined and economical to a greater or lesser extent. Probably you will also find that the business you are planning to start fits you and your personality. For example:

→ very competitive people often sell or distribute things;

→ very sensitive people often provide caring services;

→ very intuitive people often start consultancies.

Top Tip

Don't let other people tell you what your business should look like. Your business has to be a reflection of your own personality and style. It must be comfortable and made to measure. Create an enterprise that enables you to focus on your strengths.

Case study

Gary Ennis, NSDesign,

www.nsdesign.co.uk

Gary Ennis is a good example of how to align your personality and skills with your business. He set up NSDesign in 1999 and has grown the business to a team of nine. They form a one-stop shop for businesses seeking to promote and sell online through a professional web presence and social media strategy. Gary attributes ▶

his success to his determination to never forget the customer. 'However good you are,' he told me, 'unless you can communicate with and involve your customer, it's going to be a struggle.'

The decision to start a web business was not taken lightly. Trained as an architect, Gary was lecturing at a local university when the growth of the internet captured his imagination. Already something of a computer expert, he saw that creating effective websites would enable him to combine all his interests and be part of an emerging new industry.

He took the plunge and hasn't looked back once. He loves his work and is proud of what he and his team have achieved; winning numerous national business awards and building a portfolio of over 10,000 very satisfied clients. Gary regularly speaks at conferences on the subject of social media, and also to schools to promote the digital sector as a career choice.

Lifestyle	High growth
You want control over your future, a good income and to use your experience, knowledge and contacts to build a successful business.	You can see real potential for your business idea, are not afraid to take risks and want to build a business you can sell.

How entrepreneurs set goals

You have set one entrepreneurial goal already. You have decided to start the business. Established entrepreneurs break down every aspect of their enterprise (and often their life) and set goals and targets for each of them.

They will then have a number of key performance indicators (KPIs) that they monitor closely. These may include sales performance, delivery statistics and how much they owe and are owed. Software can enable these to be displayed on a single sheet or screen. Many people call this a 'business dashboard' because, like a car dashboard, it provides important information at a glance.

When you start your new business, you are unlikely to have sophisticated systems that calculate and present this information to you. You therefore need to create simple ways to measure how your business is performing. All successful entrepreneurs do this by some means or other.

Long-term goals summarise the very reasons you have for starting your business. They capture the entrepreneur's vision for the future in a way that enables them to be measured. For example:

→ 'In three years our annual sales will reach £1m and we will be making 15 per cent pre-tax profit.'

→ 'In five years we will have 35 per cent of the local market.'

→ 'In five years we will sell the business for at least £750,000.'

Probably you have set some long-term goals for your business already. It is important that they are both measurable and realistic. In fact, you will need these goals for your business plan, but more on that later.

Short-term goals/milestones are set by entrepreneurs to make sure that the business stays on track. Business growth is not constant. It will often be slow at first, then accelerate as awareness grows, customer numbers increase and confidence in the product or service builds.

In setting goals, you need to recognise this and plan accordingly. For example, here are some possible goals and milestones:

→ 'Annual sales will be:

– Year 1 – £200,000;

– Year 2 – £300,000;

– Year 3 – £450,000;

– Year 4 – £700,000;

– Year 5 – £1,000,000.'

→ 'We will win one new customer a month this year who spends at least £5,000.'

→ 'Our products will be reviewed in six trade journals this year.'

Lifestyle	High growth
Keep it simple and set a small number of high-level goals. Use these to check your vision against the plan this book will help you create.	The Business Link website, www.businesslink.gov.uk, explains KPIs in some detail. It provides a useful free download. Use it to create KPIs right now!

How to Start Your Own Business for Entrepreneurs

Case study
Gordon

Always a keen gardener, when Gordon was made redundant from the factory where he worked he decided to start a landscape gardening business. He had always done odd jobs for beer money and it seemed logical to make this his new career.

Gordon worked out that to give himself the standard of living he wanted, as well as to afford the best garden machinery, his annual sales needed to be at least £40,000. This meant working for 200 days a year at a rate of £200 a day. To achieve this rate, he knew he had to do more than just cut grass and weed borders.

Gordon decided to target high-earning private householders and offer them a service that included security fencing as well as gardening and a guaranteed daily visit when they were away from home. He would charge customers £2,000 a year for an all-in service.

Case study
Grace

When Grace moved house and could not find a reliable local window cleaner, she decided to do something about it. She knew from her job as operations manager at a busy conference centre that success was all about good customer service.

A door-to-door survey in her neighbourhood showed that her frustration was shared by many others. She started a Facebook group and soon had 200 members, many of whom were suggesting additional household services.

She left her job, recruited three excellent eastern European workers and launched her business. She plans to literally clean up in North London before expanding her business nationally.

You will find such examples of entrepreneurial activity all around you. However, it's important to set goals for your business that you are comfortable with. Do not try to copy other people.

Working out your business potential

Deep down, most of us know how large we would like our business to grow. Bigger is not necessarily better – although often it is!

As you plan to turn your business idea into reality, there are two aspects of business potential you need to consider – income and value.

Income

The starting point for most entrepreneurs is to work out how much they need to earn now and want to earn in the future. When you start your enterprise, it will take a while – perhaps months or years – before your earnings overtake the pay you'd get as an employee. Once you pass that point, your income can keep growing; something less likely to happen if you have a job!

What you need to work out is how much more you can earn working for yourself than you would if you remained employed. Even if you are not currently working – for example, because you are raising a family – entrepreneurship has to stack up financially against the alternative of getting a job.

Factors you need to consider when calculating the income potential of your new enterprise include:

→ the potential market for your products or services;

→ the cost and time involved in setting it up;

→ how much you can do yourself and how much will require staff or subcontractors;

→ how competitors will react to you entering the marketplace;

→ how quickly you will find your feet and feel comfortable growing your business.

Value

Building value into a business is where the experienced entrepreneur can score over the newcomer. Although a successful business can give you a good income and lovely lifestyle, building a business with a view to eventual sale is really the name of the game.

To think about selling your business before it has even started may seem strange. It is, however, vital to create a business that builds value and can, at the earliest possible time, continue to grow without your involvement.

Factors you need to consider when calculating the value potential of your new enterprise include:

→ intellectual property, such as patents and trademarks that can be protected;

→ momentum created by an increasing number of customers making repeat purchases;

→ opening up a new market in such a way that a large competitor chooses to buy your business rather than compete with you.

It is also important to realise that your business potential is not limited by your own skills or abilities. You simply have to be able to recruit, motivate and manage people who have the skills, abilities and perhaps contacts that your business needs. It is often said that a good entrepreneur is somebody who hires people brighter than themselves. Just because you want to start a business, it does not necessarily follow that everyone else wants to do so, too. One of the paradoxes of enterprise is that sometimes people prefer to grow a business as an employee rather than have the headache of being their own boss.

Top Tip

If you want your business to grow beyond your own abilities, you have to employ people better able and perhaps even brighter than you.

Of course, it's also important to learn what you don't know yet. Building your skills builds the potential of your business.

Frequently asked questions

Here are some typical questions asked by people about how to start a business.

Starting my own business looked like a good idea until I checked out the competition. I wonder, do I really have what it takes to be successful?
Self-doubt is natural and without it we would lack the objectivity to really make a business different from its rivals. Remember that you don't have to be better than anybody else, just different in a way that your customers recognise and value.

Everybody in the world can benefit from using the product I plan to distribute. Am I right in thinking, therefore, that my business has boundless potential and can grow into a major international corporation?
I suspect you are being encouraged to see this huge opportunity by the people whose products you are going to sell. In reality, no business can sell to everybody and you are going to need to focus on those sectors of the community you can relate to or access best. Work out how big your business needs to be to give you what you want and then plan how to achieve that.

I'm only 25. Why would I want to sell my business before I'm ready to retire?
Simple: if you can sell your business for £1 million at the age of 30 then you can invest that money in your second enterprise, which might grow even faster. Look on a business as you might look on a career. Sometimes you will move within your existing organisation, while at other times it is better to cash in and start again.

One of the big questions you may have in mind is how to find exactly the right business opportunity for you. We'll take a close look at that in the next chapter.

Key points

→ As an entrepreneur you have to see the positive in everything.

→ Your business needs to be structured to suit you, not the other way round.

→ Goals need to be both measurable and frequently measured.

→ It's OK to hire people brighter than you, providing you're the boss.

→ Structure your business so it can be sold easily, even if you don't ever sell it.

Next step

Be honest with yourself and plan your business around you, your strengths and your vision for your future.

_____

_____

_____

_____

How to find your biggest business opportunity

Chapter Two

Your first business idea may not be your best. Before you start spending money, it's wise to look at as many options as possible. That way you give yourself the best chance of creating an enterprise that makes you money and is fun to run.

> ## Don't take the bull by the horns, take him by the tail; then you can let go when you want to.

JOSH BILLINGS

The right business for you will:

→ enable you to use skills you already have and about which you are confident;

→ benefit your customers in ways they will value and can easily measure;

→ create the opportunity for you to do something about which you are passionate.

Top Tip

Be creative in how you define 'a business'. All you want is to spend time doing something you enjoy that is sustainable, financially rewarding and capable of growing to meet your long-term aspirations.

What is the right kind of business for you?

The relationship you will have with your new business is rather like the relationship many enjoy with a life partner. There are going to be ups and downs, highs and lows, thrills and spills. Giving up and walking away will be both difficult and expensive, so is best avoided. The more careful you are about choosing the right business, the more likely it is that you will enjoy more good times than bad and the relationship will last and be profitable.

Case study
Jeff

Jeff worked for a large insurance broker, specialising in company pension schemes. In his spare time he restored old cars. He began trading old car spares on eBay and soon his hobby was earning him a few thousand a year. He decided to take the plunge, leave his job and build a classic car spares business.

When he discussed the business idea with his wife she was less than convinced. She asked him how much he'd make if he simply started his own pensions brokerage. He checked out the commission rates and spoke to a couple of industry contacts.

Together the couple worked out that he could make much more money by selling pensions than from car spares. Six months later he launched his own business as a pensions broker. His income quickly rose and he had more spare cash to indulge in car restoration. He still trades car spares on eBay, but accepts that financial services are where he makes most of his money.

However much you want to do something, unless there's demand you don't have a business – you have a hobby!

Why you'll be more successful if you get this right

No one likes to have their good ideas challenged. Nevertheless, two heads are almost always better than one. In the example above, Jeff might simply have followed his heart and set up the car spares business. This would have:

→ made him less money;

→ become less appealing if now a business rather than a hobby;

→ taken him away from his easiest way to make money.

You need to be objective if you are to get this right, not to be led totally by emotion. Whatever motivates you to become an entrepreneur, your most important goal is to make money. The more profitable your business, the better able you are to:

→ spend your time doing work you enjoy;

→ invest time and money in other things that are important to you;

→ build a business you might one day be able to sell.

In other words, getting your priorities right means you create a business with the best possible chance of financial success. Profit gives you choice.

When is the right time to work this out?

Clearly you need to decide what business you're going to start before you make any significant commitment. You don't want to lock yourself into any one thing until you're totally convinced it's the right choice for you.

It's important that you look at several options and ideas before making an irreversible decision. It's equally important not to sit on the fence for too long. If you have been made redundant, for example, the longer you delay starting your business, the more of your capital you might have to spend on living expenses. You may have longer to wait before your new business delivers income.

The secret is to think before you jump, then jump in a way that is not too restricting. Inevitably your new business will evolve as it develops. You need to make sure you leave room for this to happen.

Top Tip

Some of the best businesses are those that start out doing one thing then evolve over time to retain customer appeal. For example, the popular sports drink Lucozade started out as a tonic given by mothers to their children when unwell.

Some common risks

There are some pitfalls to watch out for when you are starting a new business.

→ 'Now or never' opportunities. There are very, very few business opportunities that are so time-critical. However urgent making a decision today might appear, it always pays to avoid anyone trying to pressure you into a choice.

→ Well-meaning advice from people who have no enterprise experience. Friends often tell you about their unrealised business ambitions. It's your business; don't get talked into living out someone else's dream.

→ Anything that has never been done before. There's actually very little that is new in the world of business. As a rule, it's better to improve on what already exists than to break new ground.

Case study

Kate Hanes, Greenfinder,
http://greenfinder.co.uk

Working as a teacher in Africa, the Middle East and Australia gave Kate Hanes an insight into how green we could be. Always environmentally conscious herself, she had encouraged her friends and family to think green.

'Green living is something that I am passionate about,' Kate told me. 'In the last few years with the climate change issue hitting the headlines it seemed an ideal time to set up a green business.'

Kate was always being asked questions about recycling by friends and neighbours, so it seemed logical to set up a website advising on sustainable living. Kate sells advertising on the website and organises green events to generate income.

Kate's business combines her teaching skills with her knowledge and experience of environmental matters.

Like Kate, the more passion you feel for your business idea, the more energy you will find to drive it to reality.

Exercises to help you work it out

There are a number of factors you need to consider when trying to identify the business idea that will give you all you are looking for. These include:

→ working out objectively what you do best;

→ deciding what you enjoy doing most;

→ calculating the market opportunity with the greatest potential.

This is very different from reviewing your CV or performance review appraisals with your boss. You need to consider skills you have developed both at work and at home. A good way to work out what you enjoy doing most is to create a table like the one below. This enables you to rate tasks on a scale from 1 to 5, where 1 indicates that you don't enjoy the task at all and 5 indicates you enjoy it a lot.

HOW MUCH YOU ENJOY DOING THIS

	1	*2*	*3*	*4*	*5*
Preparing food					X
Dealing with customers					X
Teaching			X		
Dealing with suppliers			X		
Working in the evening	X				
Being part of a large team		X			
Working alone				X	

The table above was filled in by Penny, a lecturer at a catering college. She used to run a restaurant, but after having children she no longer liked the unsocial hours and so got a teaching job.

You can see, however, that Penny misses food preparation and dealing with customers. She doesn't mind teaching but clearly is no longer motivated by it.

After doing this exercise with a close friend, they came up with the idea of opening a sandwich shop. This would provide the customer contact and hands-on food preparation that Penny was most missing.

However, just wanting to do something is not a good enough reason to actually do it. There has to be a market ready and willing to welcome your product or service. The world is full of businesses established because the owner wanted to do something. Many do not succeed because potential customers do not view the new enterprise with the same enthusiasm as the founder.

Checking out your market opportunity so that you do not open a business that nobody wants to patronise is covered in Chapter Three. Here the focus is on you and your personal ambitions and expectations.

What about some alternatives?

Let's continue with our example of Penny, the college lecturer, considering opening a sandwich shop. Most people, having thought of the business that seems to meet their personal needs, look no further. They simply go out and seek the best place to start the business of which they first thought. But there are always alternatives. For example, Penny's options include:

→ a sandwich shop, either on the high street or in a business area;

→ a sandwich round visiting people at work or even at home;

→ setting up a café inside a large corporate headquarters;

→ a snack foods factory wholesaling to corner shops and filling stations;

→ an event catering company, which would free her from the routine of having to open a shop every single morning.

Your turn

To make sure that you consider all the alternatives, here are three simple exercises that will help you. Remember that, unless prompted, you cannot possibly know what you do not yet know. You have to start with the obvious and then move sideways to create a broader spectrum. Grab some paper and a pen so that you can record your answers.

Exercise 1: who else does that?

In the middle of a piece of paper, write down the principal activity or business idea you have decided is best for you. Next, in a circle around it, write some other businesses that contain the same activities. Then create a wider circle containing less obvious examples. For example, if you started with gardening, your word group might look like this:

> *Green burials cemetery   Exhibition floristry*
> *Propagating house plants   Market gardening*
> *Pitch and putt course*   **Gardening**   *Herb growing/drying*
> *Grounds maintenance   Landscape design*
> *Rural crafts centre   Tourist attraction*

Can you see how – by starting with what you want to do – the wider you go, the more options you discover? Each option can then be explored in more detail to see which one offers you the profit and lifestyle you seek. Look beyond the obvious to identify your biggest opportunity.

Exercise 2: where does this happen?

Most people starting a business are going to operate in one particular marketplace. If your customers will visit your premises, this is a physical marketplace constrained by geography. If you're going to supply a specialist service to transport companies, then you might cover the country but only deal with one market sector, say tanker fleets.

Now repeat Exercise 1, but this time looking at *where* not *what*. The example opposite is by a software developer, brainstorming the types of location or setting where his voice recognition programme might be used:

Vending machines   *Theme parks*
Disability charities   *Security equipment industry*
School computers   **Voice recognition software**   *Office computers*
Leisure industry   *Household appliance makers*
Information kiosks   *Language schools*

This exercise helps you to look outside the industry sectors you already know and understand. It can help you to list the potential markets for your business, ready for you to explore and evaluate in the next chapter.

Top Tip

One product or service can have a far higher value and command a higher price in some markets than others. For example, you pay more for an ice-cream on the beach than in the supermarket. It makes sense to focus on your most lucrative markets first.

Exercise 3: what is the opposite of what I want to do most?

In this final exercise, you need to explore the very things you do not want to do. This is about you – not your skills or experience. For example, you might decide:

→ you hate late nights;

→ you don't think you would enjoy cold-calling;

→ you get bored doing the same thing week in, week out;

→ you like to have the flexibility to take the odd afternoon off.

Then look at the business you are thinking of starting and consider the extent to which it provides the opposite to what you do not want to do. For example:

→ if you hated late nights you would not run a bar;

→ if you don't like to cold-call, you might prefer retailing to door-to-door selling;

→ if you get bored quickly, you want lots of new customers rather than providing the same service to the same customers for many years;

→ if you want flexibility, you don't want to have your diary full of commitments for months into the future.

This exercise will help you to see the impact of the business you are considering on your preferred way of life. It may seem trivial to look at personal preferences in this way, but creating the lifestyle you want is one of the key reasons for starting your own business in the first place.

Lifestyle	High growth
These questions are most relevant if you are starting a business that will make you happy.	You may be willing to make some personal compromises to create an enterprise with the potential you seek.

Frequently asked questions

Here are some of the questions that people often ask when considering what business to start after reading this book.

My partner thinks this is silly and that I should just get a better job. Who's right?
Everyone is different and it could be that what excites you about entrepreneurship terrifies your partner. Make it a challenge to create a plan that reassures even your partner that you are going to succeed.

I have done the exercises in this chapter but the business I really want to start is so specialist, where will I find customers?
The rest of this book will help you to work out how to find customers. What you need to appreciate right now is that the internet will probably help you to do this. More important is to recognise that, in general, specialist business start-ups do better than those that simply try to meet everyone's needs. You're probably on the right track. ▶

I've read this chapter twice and am still short of good ideas. What should I do now?

To trigger your inspiration, take some time off and look around. Visit a town you do not know and look at the businesses there. You will see plenty you don't want to copy, but try to build a list that contains elements of the businesses you encounter you might be good at. Some of the best businesses are started by people who see something being done badly and decide to do it better. You might be one of those people.

I actually now have too many ideas and don't know which to do first! How can I decide?

Listen to your instinct. Which idea does your heart tell you will be the most successful? Also look at which you think will be the easiest to start and will have the greatest potential. It is important to be focused on just one idea when you come to write your plan.

If you're not sure yet whether you've found the right business, the next chapter will help you to evaluate possibilities in more detail.

Key points

→ Your first idea may not be your best – look around before committing.

→ Listen to those around you, but remember that it is your decision.

→ Be objective and look at all your skills and interests.

→ Don't be persuaded to rush into something that you have not checked out.

→ Exploring the ridiculous can help you find the obvious.

→ Remember that this will not be easy, so take your time and get it right.

Next step

Focus on what you do well, know well and, deep down, makes sense to you. That's where you'll find your greatest opportunity.

_____

_____

_____

_____

How to be really sure your business idea will fly

Chapter Three

You have already explored your business idea, but have you covered all the angles? Most people test out their new business idea on family and friends. Their feedback is important but not necessarily unbiased. You owe it to yourself to take an objective look at your business proposition before you fully commit to the project.

It is the new and different that is always most vulnerable to market research. MALCOLM GLADWELL

What research do you need to do?

Market research is a double-edged sword. Too little and you run the risk of investing in a flawed concept. Too much and you can be overwhelmed by conflicting data and never start at all.

As a new entrepreneur, you will also feel a strong emotional attachment to your business idea. This is good as you have to champion it strongly to get the enterprise off the ground. It can also cloud your judgment if your research tells you what you really don't want to hear.

The following are some of the things you should research before starting your new business.

Your motivation

Starting a business is a very personal journey to make. Research, of course, inevitably focuses on the world outside your head, but that doesn't mean you should neglect to consider what's going on inside your head. Your motivation for starting an enterprise has to be factored in to your research. For example, are you:

→ angry – and determined to compete with someone you feel deserves more competition;

→ frustrated – because you feel you can do better than what's already available;

→ hurt – because you've lost your job and want to prove your worth to others;

→ impatient – and unwilling to simply grow your career working for someone else?

How to Start Your Own Business for Entrepreneurs

These often powerful emotional drivers are what motivate us to overcome obstacles and achieve success. You need to recognise and focus them effectively. Your business has to become the vehicle for your emotional as well as your economic success.

Whatever else your research reveals, remember that the enterprise you create has to motivate you. Otherwise it's just another job, this time with no guarantees and a very demanding boss!

Lifestyle	High growth
For you, research is very much an emotional exercise. You want to do something and will research to justify or adapt your vision.	Money is more important for you. Research might take you away from your first idea. However, don't lose sight of the importance of an emotional connection with your new enterprise. It makes you more resilient!

Market size

How many people already use what you propose to supply? This can be straightforward if, for example, you are going to be a haulier, as you can easily find out the volume of freight shipped by road. If, however, you are breaking new ground, perhaps providing training to potential stand-up comics, then determining market size is almost impossible. You just don't know how many people fancy themselves as comedians!

Market trends

Many once-big names in industry have disappeared because they continued to supply a declining market. For example, Richard Garrett was a very successful nineteenth-century maker of steam traction engines. When diesel tractors came along, the company did not diversify quickly enough and quite literally ran out of steam.

However, your business does not have to be supplying a growing market. Sometimes a declining market can give you as much business as you need, as long as there is little competition. As others diversify away from a market, you remain as a specialist supplier. Thatchers are an example of this, able to charge a premium price for their reed or straw roofing.

Market analysis

It is almost impossible to start a business that is truly unique. Almost everything has been done before or is already being done by others. Your research needs to help you understand how what you're going to offer is different from what's already available. This is really important and makes it far easier to describe your offer. For example, Domino's Pizza and Pizza Express both sell pizza. One specialises in delivery, the other in providing a complete dining experience.

Top Tip

Define your business by the better-known enterprises that are similar. This highlights your niche market in a way others will easily see.

Case study
Roland Schreiber, Expresso,
www.expresso-online.co.uk

Roland Schreiber runs Expresso, a popular independent coffee shop in Norwich city centre. He competes with all the major multiple coffee shop outlets and attracts his customers because he is different. He allows artists to exhibit on the café walls, so there is always something new to see. He also serves every cup of coffee with a chocolate wafer in the saucer. Both are small things, but they make the customer experience different enough to attract customers.

How to balance your instinct with market research

Your instinct will give you a good feel for what will work and what won't, but instinct alone is not enough. Before investing money, you will require hard facts and evidence of need for what you're going to do.

How to Start Your Own Business for Entrepreneurs

Let's assume you are going to open a vegetarian restaurant and you want to find out if the facts support your instincts. Here's how you could do it.

Your instincts suggest:	Check it out like this:
people want to eat healthily	look in people's supermarket trolleys
vegetarianism is gaining ground	read press and survey reports online
local restaurants are not vegetarian-friendly	look at menus and ask in a few places why they have such a limited veggie menu
there's a local demand	do a street survey*

* Check with your local council before doing a street survey. You may need permission.

The risk of relying purely on instinct is that you are looking to justify your idea. You are seeking out support (which is important) and might not be as objective as you should. Your instinctive research, however, quick and rough though it is, will at least allow you to become more comfortable talking to others about your business idea – in particular, talking to people you don't know. It's a short step from selling and therefore important to do.

Top Tip

When you survey people to identify demand, note also what those who support your idea have in common. Perhaps they are all young or old or of a type. This will help you later when it comes to branding and adding customer appeal.

The 'So what?' game

One way to really test your business idea is to challenge it. You can do this by playing the 'So what?' game. It's basically a conversation with yourself, but it helps to write it down.

Ask yourself a series of questions about your enterprise and answer each with 'So what?' Then go on to justify the idea. It's rather like the way a child won't take no for an answer, simply responding to each point the parent makes with 'Why?' Eventually the parent gives in, but you must not.

Here's an example.

> *'I'm going to open a vegetarian restaurant.'*
>
> So what? Who's going to go there?
>
> *'Well, more people are eating vegetarian now – it's so healthy.'*
>
> So what? Since when did people choose to do healthy things?
>
> *'But it makes sense to be healthy and there's lots of evidence that says meat eating is in decline.'*
>
> So what? You're talking about intellectuals, most won't bother.
>
> *'That's as may be, but there is no vegetarian restaurant in this city so what business there is will come our way.'*
>
> So what? If there was a demand, there would already be one.

At this point, you should have a few doubts. Is there a market? Has someone else tried and failed? How much of this plan is your personal idealism and how much does it make sound commercial sense? All these are questions to ask yourself as you begin to check out your opportunity.

Quick and easy ways to check out your business idea

The more you research your business idea before starting out, the better your chances of success. However, it is wise to keep a sense of proportion and not get bogged down in detailed statistics. Here are the key factors to consider.

Market size

You need to be totally confident that there is a market out there for what you are planning to do. That means people:

→ need what you provide and are currently not supplied with it;

→ buy what you do elsewhere and are likely to change;

→ are not yet 'in the market' but are likely to become interested.

How to Start Your Own Business for Entrepreneurs

To determine your market size you also need to work out realistically how big a territory your business can service. For example:

→ How far will people travel to visit your shop?

→ How large are the online communities you can service via the internet (and what are the physical constraints that might limit delivery)?

In some markets this will be easy, while in others it will be virtually impossible. For example:

→ an artificial limb maker can access health statistics that accurately predict the number of amputations carried out each year;

→ a maker of snack foods faces a far more complicated exercise as demand is largely stimulated by advertising and the way the products are displayed in supermarkets.

To work out your potential market size, consider all or some of the following activities.

→ Look online for relevant published statistics.

→ Look at the advertising 'media packs' of publications read by your target audience (these usually define market size and state their share of it to justify the rates they charge).

→ Visit the places your target customers go and literally see who's there.

→ Look for online communities frequented by your target customers.

→ Get copies of the annual reports of listed suppliers to your marketplace. These may define market size and the narrative might also reveal market issues you are not currently aware of.

Top Tip

University students are good at research. Consider recruiting one via your local university careers office to carry out a research project for you.

Market trends

You don't need a growing market to succeed but it helps. All markets are constantly evolving. This is due to:

→ changing user behaviour (e.g. people are buying smaller cars now);

→ fashion (e.g. more men are growing beards);

→ legislation (e.g. public buildings have to be wheelchair accessible);

→ economic factors (e.g. rising metal prices make recycling more profitable).

These trends might influence your decision about the products or services you are going to market. For example, it's as easy to distribute beard trimmers as electric razors. You might give both equal focus in recognition of the trend towards beard wearing.

To work out how your market is changing, consider all or some of the following activities.

→ Read trade journals and see what's being hailed as new.

→ Visit relevant exhibitions and see what's being promoted.

→ Search online for new patents/technology in your sector.

→ Ask journalists who write about your marketplace (buy them lunch).

→ Talk to academics and researchers working in your market sector.

→ Carry out (or commission) a consumer survey.

Market analysis

Trends show you where a market is going. Analysis helps you to find your place within the marketplace. Inevitably you will be competing with existing providers. You need to balance your understanding of market size and trends against what's already there. From this you will pick out the ways in which you can be different from your rivals.

The way you do this is by looking hard at your competitors. Work out their strengths and weaknesses. How have they become complacent and not moved with the times? What are their specialities and how might yours differ?

How to Start Your Own Business for Entrepreneurs

Your activities might include:

→ reviewing competitor websites and literature;

→ mystery shopping and buying from your rivals;

→ interviewing your target customers about their buying experiences.

Top Tip

The UK government publishes a lot of statistical data under a number of themes. This is useful for your market research. It is also very credible if quoted in your business plan. See **www.statistics.gov.uk**

Remember that you want to differentiate yourself clearly from others. This makes marketing easier and helps customers see the value of giving you a try. Sometimes this will mean changing your plan slightly, perhaps specialising in an area you've found is not well covered elsewhere. Conversely, you might simply decide to offer the same products or services as everyone else, but make the customer experience more pleasurable.

For a more detailed guide through the entire marketing process, see *Marketing for Entrepreneurs* by Jurgen Wolff (Prentice Hall Business, 2009).

What your bank manager will want to know

If you need to borrow money to start your business, your bank manager will have many questions. Even if you don't need to borrow money, it's good to behave as if you do. The discipline of preparing your plan for scrutiny by a professional banker is a good one. In fact, you need to appreciate that when a bank manager says no, they might well be doing you a favour. Just as they don't want to lose their money, they don't really want to see you lose your own either.

Most banks provide template business plans and lots of other useful tools. These are there to help you, as well as to recruit you as a customer. Most are, by necessity, complex as they have to cover a wide range of situations. Don't be afraid to miss out the stuff that doesn't seem important to your situation (your bank manager will soon tell you if it is!).

Above all else, a bank manager wants to determine that:

→ you understand the business sector you're entering;

→ you have the energy, enthusiasm and determination to succeed;

→ you've done your own research and written your own plan, even if this proves to be just a starting point;

→ your personal financial situation is not too precarious;

→ your family is right behind you and supports your plan.

Frequently asked questions

Here are some typical questions asked by people researching their business opportunity.

I've worked in the industry for years and know the ropes. I'm only doing this because my employer went bust. Why do I need to do research?
Well, how about because your employer did go bust! Clearly things were not right and your view of the industry might be undesirably biased by the organisation you've just left. Take a fresh look and see what it's really like.

My business idea feels right. I know there's no one doing it yet, but that's because no one has yet had the courage to stand up and be counted. Isn't that enough to be getting on with?
Beware of becoming a martyr to a lost cause. There's usually a good reason why there is no one already doing something. Often someone's tried and failed or the marketplace is not ready yet. If you take one tip from this book, let it be that you should always let others be the pioneers and break new ground. You can then follow when it's safe and provide customers with choice.

I have a large redundancy cheque and a small pension. The kids have left home so, really, do I need to do all this stuff? Can't I afford simply to tick along?
Sure, but if you're not in business to make a profit then you're simply taking up a hobby. Take your business seriously and, yes, do what you're going to enjoy, but make sure you're properly rewarded for what you do. Remember, money means choice and you don't know what challenges await you later in life.

In the next chapter you'll find out how to structure your business to help ensure that it will be a success.

Key points

→ Research alone won't make a business successful. You have to exploit the potential you discover.

→ Market trends can be more significant than market size. It's the potential, not the past, that's important.

→ Banks and other lenders need reassurance that you know what you're doing as well as where you're going.

Next step

Reflect on your business idea and ask yourself if it really feels right. Make sure you're following your vision, not someone else's!

_____

_____

_____

_____

Business type – what's possible

You should now have some clear ideas forming about what you want your business to do. In Chapter Five we'll look at the different legal structures you might adopt. But before you look at how you're going to structure your enterprise, you need to consider the range of business types on offer.

Few start-up books will present these as a separate topic, even though it can be bewildering. To steer you away from confusion and help you better understand some of the opportunities you may encounter, let's look at some of them now.

You must do the thing you think you cannot do.

ELEANOR ROOSEVELT

Starting from scratch

This is what most of us do. You have the idea, set up the enterprise and open for business. In fact this book has been written with this route in mind. When you start from scratch, everything about your enterprise is going to be new and so everything has to be done.

What's good about this is that you will reap all of the rewards because, providing you retain 100 per cent ownership of the venture, it is all your own idea and work. Inevitably starting from scratch doesn't create a totally unique business. For example, all bakeries bake bread, even though the one you set up might make cupcakes, too!

People who set up a business from scratch will often be:

→ visionary, able to see what they are going to create;

→ robust, with the strength to overcome the obstacles and make it happen;

→ resilient, able to get by financially while their business gets off the ground.

Buying an existing business

This is also an option. How to buy an existing business is covered in Chapter Seven. The benefit of buying an established enterprise is that you bypass many of the start-up challenges. An existing business will already have:

→ products and services;

→ customers and market reputation;

→ assets and liabilities.

Most importantly, an existing business has momentum. Even if it has slipped into decline, perhaps because the owner has been ill or distracted, you can be trading from day one.

People who buy an existing business will often be:

→ experienced in the market sector they are buying into;

→ financially able to invest;

→ more comfortable developing an existing enterprise than starting from scratch.

Top Tip

Just as the business sector you enter will depend on your interests and experience, so the business type you choose will depend on your personality and the size of your comfort zone.

Lifestyle	High growth
Buying an existing business can save you the hassle of building from scratch. Try to link the price you pay to future performance. You'll need your cash for working capital.	Remember that McDonald's was an existing small business when Ray Kroc came along and saw the potential. See what's possible, not just what exists.

Multi-level marketing and direct selling

Most of us at some time in our lives have been approached by someone seeking to recruit us into their 'network'. Multi-level, network marketing and party plan are commonly used terms to describe businesses that sell direct to the consumer though a network of associates. Avon, Amway, Herbalife and The Utility Warehouse are all well-known, respected examples.

The business model succeeds because people sell to friends and neighbours – people they know. They also have the opportunity to introduce new agents to the network. To encourage people to support those they introduce, they receive a commission on the sales generated by what is called their 'downline'. Direct selling companies are usually big on training and have proven methodologies that, if followed, can enable you to build both immediate and residual income.

The benefit of joining a direct selling organisation is that you:

→ distribute branded products and services provided by a reliable, proven supplier;

→ receive full training and ongoing support;

→ need very little, if any, money to get started.

You also need to bear in mind that not everyone holds the direct selling sector in high esteem. This is for two reasons:

→ it used to be less well regulated and some people felt they were over-promised;

→ it succeeds because someone you know invites you to be a customer; some folk find this a little too direct for comfort!

People who become self-employed with a direct selling organisation are often:

→ looking for a second income that one day can grow to become their main occupation;

→ happier within a structured business environment;

→ team players.

For more information, see The Direct Selling Association, at **http://dsa.org.uk**

Case study

Karen Rhys-Gill, Avon,
www.avon.uk.com

Karen joined Avon when she moved house and found there was nobody covering her new neighbourhood. She works from home and enjoys meeting lots of new people. 'It's very family-friendly,' she said. 'I never thought I would have a job that I enjoy so much.'

At the end of her first year, Karen was able to take her son to France for three weeks to visit his grandparents. She'd also earned enough to make some improvements to her new house.

Buying a franchise

The word 'franchise' can cover several business models. Its most common meaning in the business start-up world is to describe a 'business format franchise'. This is where you buy into a proven business model and benefit from the reputation and expertise of an established organisation. For example, many fast food restaurants are franchises.

When you buy a fast food franchise you agree to invest in and open an outlet in a new location. You commit to using the franchisor's branding, to sell their products at the prices they set. You have less freedom than with your own concept, but the huge benefit of being an established brand from day one. Imagine the difference between opening an independent burger restaurant and a new McDonald's outlet. You don't need to guess which would be packed with customers on opening day!

The benefit of buying into a franchise is that you:

→ distribute branded products and services provided by a reliable, proven supplier;

→ receive full training and ongoing support;

→ can benefit from special bank deals negotiated by the franchisor with leading banks.

People who buy a franchise are often:

→ looking for a business they know will give them income from the beginning;

→ fortunate enough to have money to invest, perhaps a redundancy cheque;

→ happy to follow a proven methodology rather than try to reinvent the wheel.

For more information, see The British Franchise Association at **www. thebfa.org**

Case study

Jayesh Patel, Signs Express, Twickenham,
www.signsexpress.co.uk/branch/49/twickenham

Jayesh worked in IT before deciding to buy a Signs Express franchise. He liked the Signs Express business model. The company has a number of large corporate clients, served locally by individual franchisees. Jayesh could see how, in London, supplying big name customers would help him differentiate himself from the many small, independent sign companies in the area.

Now running for eight years, Jayesh's franchise has grown to employ four people. He enjoys the mix of technology, management and sales his business gives him. In particular, he enjoys the support provided by Signs Express.

His advice to you if you're considering buying a franchise is this: 'Franchises work because you buy into and then follow what has been proved to work. You need to be enterprising, but not so entrepreneurial that you'll feel the need to change things. Franchising works if you do what works!'

Being a broker or sales agent

Some of the best innovations have been the result of a product that is established in one market being introduced to another. For example, wheelie bins were developed for domestic waste handling, but make great portable feed storage bins for farmers. If your background was in agricultural feed and you became self-employed, you might well have made the connection between your bin at home and the problem farmers have keeping vermin out of animal feed.

I have done this myself recently. Having worked for a couple of years in the park home industry some 25 years ago, I knew where to look when confronted with a community shop project struggling to raise the cash to buy a building to convert into a shop. Now they need to raise less money because I'm organising a factory-built shop, made to order by a park home manufacturer.

In this personal example, I know that the community shop project would never have realised that a factory-built shop was an option for them. Equally, being focused on making factory-built retirement 'bungalows', the park home manufacturer would never have discovered this new market.

The benefit of negotiating an agency relationship is that you:

→ can enter a market you could not raise the cash to enter on your own;

→ are up and running as soon as you've agreed and signed an agency agreement;

→ can adapt quickly if market conditions change.

People who become agents in this way are often:

→ from a sales and marketing background;

→ good at building and maintaining relationships;

→ creative thinkers.

Frequently asked questions

Here are some typical questions asked by new entrepreneurs about the financial aspects of starting their businesses.

My boss wants to retire and is asking me to buy the business. Is this a good idea?

There's a lot to be said for buying into a business you know and understand. As your boss has good knowledge of you, you are well placed to negotiate the best deal for both parties. Remember that, as they are retiring, it might be beneficial for you to buy the business in stages. Make sure, too, that you both get independent advice. You don't want to find yourself paying over the odds if it's a business that would otherwise be difficult to sell.

A friend has just signed up with a direct selling company and wants me to sign up, too. She is very ambitious and expects to be able to make a very good living within six months. I hate my job and want to go it alone. Should I accept her invitation?

Direct selling organisations work by building networks of people like you and your friend. Their strength is that product sales are made by people selling to people they know. Their weakness is that it can take quite a long time and a lot of determination to build a direct selling business. Give it a try by all means and see where it leads, but don't chuck in the day job until you're earning enough to replace the income you'll lose.

I've just been to a big franchise exhibition and am confused by the vast range of opportunities on offer. I have the money to invest and like the comradeship I think I'll find as a franchisee rather than going it alone. Help!

Pick a number of franchise opportunities you think you'll enjoy and ask to meet some existing franchisees. As well as those you'll be introduced to, find some on ▶

your own and give them a ring or visit. It's really important to join a franchise you will enjoy, as otherwise the long hours and commitment demanded will make it feel like you've simply gone and got another job.

Key points

→ There is a range of business types to consider.

→ Remember that if you're being asked to invest, it's vital to take independent advice.

→ No business opportunity will get you rich quick. Make sure you can fund yourself as you build your new venture.

Next step

There is no right or wrong answer to the 'Which business type?' question. Make sure, as you research, you look at the potential of each opportunity. That's what matters most.

_____

_____

_____

_____

Business structure – building in room to grow

Chapter Five

The most important thing to remember when structuring your new business is that you must keep its finances separate from your own. Even if your enterprise is little more than a profitable hobby, it is still worthwhile keeping separate accounts and having a separate bank account. Your business needs to have its own identity, too, separate from your own. Let's consider how you can choose the right structure for your business.

Good order is the foundation of all things.

EDMUND BURKE

The three main business structures

There are essentially only three structures a business can have. These are:

→ sole trader – where you operate as a self-employed person;

→ partnership – two or more self-employed people working together;

→ limited company – a separate legal entity you can own and be employed by.

Choosing the right structure is not straightforward. Much depends on you, your aspirations and your attitude to things such as risk and taxation.

Top Tip

You want to get the right structure from the start. Most accountants will give you a free initial consultation. This is because they want to recruit you as a client. Use this opportunity to discuss your plans with a professional adviser.

Sole trader

This is the term used to describe a self-employed person. You have to account for your income and business expenses on your annual tax return and pay tax on your profits twice a year. It is essential to keep your business transactions separate from your personal transactions.

How to Start Your Own Business for Entrepreneurs

If you have regular customers, you (and they) need to make sure that the tax authorities can't mistake you for an employee. In some business sectors such as construction and IT, this is really important because they employ many temporary staff that the tax authorities prefer to consider as employed.

To be considered self-employed rather than employed it helps to be able to show that you are:

→ working for more than one customer;

→ clearly in control of what you do and when and how you do it;

→ providing your own tools and equipment;

→ able to subcontract or hire your own staff to do the work;

→ responsible for correcting any mistakes you make.

This can be a particular issue if you leave an organisation's employment and continue to work for them in a freelance capacity. Many people do this as it makes good sense for all concerned, but you do need to win additional clients within a few months or questions might be asked.

Top Tip

If you are leaving employment to go it alone, even if as the result of redundancy, don't overlook the fact that your old boss might become your first client. You'd be surprised how many people got started because their old boss gave them work in the early days of their business.

The pros to being a sole trader:

→ bookkeeping is relatively simple;

→ you pay your tax twice a year;

→ business-related costs and expenses can be set against tax.

The cons to being a sole trader:

→ you might need to incorporate (set up a limited company) later;

→ you can be held personally liable for any debts;

→ some organisations prefer to deal with a limited company.

Partnership

This essentially is two or more self-employed people working together. You can have differing shares in the partnership and pay tax on your share of the partnership profits. Partners can sell their share and new partners can buy in. It's a flexible structure. It is also possible to create a 'limited liability partnership' that gives each partner, as the name suggests, limited liability in the event of the partnership going bust or being sued.

Partnerships are:

→ the structure usually adopted by professional practices;

→ popular with husbands and wives who work together.

The pros:

→ bookkeeping remains relatively simple;

→ you can recruit an investor who is not active in the business (a sleeping partner);

→ business-related costs and expenses can be set against tax.

The cons:

→ you can be held 'jointly and severally liable' for debts (in other words, if one partner defaults the others have to pay their share);

→ the partnership must be dissolved if a partner dies or becomes bankrupt;

→ you need a lawyer to help you put together a partnership agreement.

Limited company

This has a separate and distinct legal entity from the people who own and operate it. It brings both benefits and restrictions. A limited company is the structure to go for if you:

→ plan to build a significant business;

→ want to raise money from investors;

→ expect to sell your business one day.

The pros:

→ you can issue and sell shares to raise investment;

→ the business is easier to sell (in part or entirely);

→ your personal liability (as a director) is limited.

The cons:

→ bookkeeping is more complex and your accountancy bills higher;

→ lenders and some suppliers will probably demand a personal guarantee, negating the benefits of limited liability;

→ there are higher costs associated with setting it up.

Lifestyle	High growth
If the risks are modest the most advantageous business structure for most is to be a sole trader or partner.	All high-growth businesses incorporate (become limited companies) so that investors can easily take shares in the business. Often they then go on to 'float' and become 'public limited companies' (PLC). This enables almost anyone to invest and buy shares. It also enables the founders to take some profit by selling some of their shares.

Case study

James Bowles, Bowles Print Management UK,
www.bpm-UK.co.uk

James Bowles developed a passion for print and design while working for a Sussex-based printer. When his employer went bust he decided to realise his ambition and start his own print broker business.

That was in 2007 and bpm-uk is still going strong. James works with clients locally, regionally and nationally, providing them with a complete print and design service, working with tight budgets to achieve the best quality.

'Being self-employed is challenging but liberating,' James told me. 'I am content with being a sole trader at the moment. I have a great work–life balance and I am able to work on many different projects, I have low overheads and business is tightly controlled within budgets.'

'I have been lucky to work on some amazing projects like printing welcome banners for Take That, Bon Jovi and Pink and I have worked with AEG Live and Live Nation. I have also added a social media side to the business, which has brought in an extra revenue stream.'

Why is it important to get this right?

Setting up your business is a clear signal to everyone that you are serious. This is not just an idea or dream, but something you're actually going to do. Choosing the right structure forces you to think about your longer-term goals. Will you be seeking investors? Will you work alone or with others? Are you hoping to sell your business one day?

It can also be very complicated to change the structure of a business once it's up and running. You really do need to take advice and get this right first time.

The person you are most likely to ask is an accountant.

How to choose an accountant

An accountant is in business to make money. They will have worked out the type of client they work with best and will hopefully set out their stall to attract the kind of business they want.

Accountants charge for their time by the hour, although many will negotiate an annual fee and allow you to pay this in monthly instalments.

When searching for an accountant, look for:

→ someone you can trust and relate to;

→ a firm with clients like you;

→ expertise in your type of business;

→ enthusiasm to welcome you as a new client.

Most accountants win new clients by introduction. Ask people whose opinion you respect to recommend a firm to you. Ask them to explain why they are happy to introduce them to you.

Other business structures

There are actually more than three possible structures you can adopt, although the three already mentioned are by far the most common. This is why it really is so important to take advice. This is particularly true if you are setting up a charity or social enterprise: there are specialist legal structures designed to meet the specific needs of both. For example, the most common is a **Community Interest Company (CIC)**.

Many social and community enterprises are structured as CICs. Essentially this is a limited liability company that embeds within its governance documents rules that:

- → define the social purpose for which it was set up (community of interest);
- → locks assets to avoid profiteering by shareholders;
- → restricts profit distribution so that most is reinvested in its social purpose.

Because they have less profit opportunity than ordinary limited companies, CICs can attract grant funding. This and the legal transparency of purpose are the main reasons they are set up.

How to set up your business, step by step

Let's assume you have a name for your business (there are tips on choosing a name in Chapter Thirteen). You have also decided what structure to go for, having hopefully taken some good advice from an accountant or other respected business adviser. Now you need to set up the business. Where do you start?

Step 1: Banking

A good first step is to open a business bank account. This is vital as you must keep your business and personal banking separate. It is also really exciting to see your new chequebook and paying-in book. It brings what has so far been a vision into reality.

When choosing your business bank, think about the following.

- → Using a different bank from the one you bank with personally. They might not be the best for your business and many entrepreneurs prefer to keep their personal finances totally separate.
- → Branch location, as you'll have to pay in cheques and possibly cash.
- → The quality of their online banking offer.
- → The account manager who'll be looking after you – will you get on?

Banks are different. You need to choose one that fits with your business aspiration. They fall into four broad categories.

→ **Simple** These banks specialise in offering great value to small businesses that require no more than a simple banking service. If you keep your account in credit, make only a modest number of transactions and don't want to borrow (much), they are perfect.

→ **Standard** These are the main high street banks. They'll offer you an enticing array of incentives to open a business account and you'll have an account manager you can talk to. Most people start with one of these. As your business grows, they will be able to deal with your changing needs and pass you on to more senior colleagues able to lend larger amounts.

→ **Boutique** There is a growing number of boutique banks. These are often non-British and pride themselves on their ability to configure tailor-made banking arrangements for people with non-standard needs. They are often the best bet if you are already wealthy or need to structure your personal and business debt in a particular way.

→ **Faith** There are also specialist banks that structure their banking services to comply with your faith or moral stance. The Islamic Bank of Britain, for example, provides Sharia-compliant banking that enables Muslim entrepreneurs to do business free of conflict with their religious beliefs. There are also banks that have more 'ethical' investment policies than others, as well as banks that specialise in social enterprises.

Whichever bank you choose, they will ask you for various facts, figures and documents, particularly if you're setting up a limited company. This gives you a useful checklist to work from. Fact is, the information the bank will ask for is also useful for you!

Top Tip

If you're starting out as a limited liability company, you'll need to set this up before opening a bank account. Your bank will need a copy of the 'certificate of incorporation'. This arrives from Companies House when your company has been set up.

Step 2: Paperwork

The paperwork you need depends on the business structure you're setting up. As you might expect, the more complicated the structure, the more paperwork you'll need.

→ **Sole trader** The only paperwork you need to become a sole trader is your chequebook, paying-in book and ideally some business cards or flyers. It really can be as simple as that.

→ **Partnership** You need no more paperwork to form a partnership than you do to start up as a sole trader. However, you would be well advised to pay a solicitor to draw up a simple partnership agreement. This defines what happens if your circumstances change. Even life partners who start a business together often choose to have a formal partnership agreement. If nothing else, it helps you both to see the business as something separate from your relationship.

> **Top Tip**
>
> Always have a simple, legal partnership agreement, even if your business partner is your best friend. It will avoid arguments or time-consuming negotiations later on.

→ **Limited company** A limited company is a separate legal entity. How it will be governed and why it exists are defined in the 'memo and arts' (Memorandum of Understanding and Articles of Association, see below). Your bank will also require you to pass some company resolutions appointing it as your banking institution. Fortunately, all these rather complicated forms are very much the same. You can download model 'memo and arts' from a number of websites. Helpfully these highlight the bits that matter, which may well need to be different for your company. Banks are also helpful, in that they give you pro forma 'resolution' forms to sign. It's not as difficult as it sounds.

Additional considerations for a limited company

Limited companies have to be registered (at Companies House) because they are separate legal entities. They also need to have a 'memo and arts'. These are two legal documents that define the way the company is set up and the parameters within which it will operate. Companies House will not register your company and a bank will not open an account without these documents.

There are several ways to set up a limited company, including the following.

→ **Specialist registration agents** You see their adverts in business classifieds, offering a 'limited company for £50' and so on. These can be good value, but you need to be sure the standard 'memo and arts' they use does not restrict you. It costs money to change these documents.

→ **Your accountant** This will cost more but probably work out cheaper in the long run. Your accountant will make sure the paperwork covers your specific needs. They will also register themselves with the tax authorities as your agent. This means they automatically get copies of all tax correspondence – one less thing for you to worry about.

→ **Yourself** It is possible to do all this yourself direct with Companies House. However, your time can probably be better spent elsewhere.

You will also need to look at insurance. This is covered in Chapter Twenty-three.

Step 3: Tax authorities

If you're employed, you will currently be paying tax on your income or will have done so recently. You need to tell your tax office (or have your accountant tell them) that your situation has changed. If you are setting up a limited company, you will be employed by it. Otherwise you'll be effectively self-employed. You will have to complete an annual personal tax return or delegate this to your accountant.

You will also need to tell your local authority if you are occupying business premises so that you can pay business rates.

Finally, you will need to register for value-added tax (VAT) if you expect your turnover to exceed the annual threshold. There are two key points to note about VAT.

→ You can voluntarily register if your turnover is below the threshold. This enables you to reclaim the tax paid on purchases, but you must also charge the tax on your sales.

→ You can reclaim the VAT on some of your set-up costs, such as computers, equipment and so on, when you make your first VAT return, even if you were not registered for VAT when the purchases were made. (There is a time limit for this; for the latest regulations, or to register for VAT, visit **www.hmrc.gov.uk**).

Top Tip

If you sell to the general public, who cannot reclaim the VAT you charge, it might be more profitable for you to keep your annual sales below the threshold for VAT registration. This can give you a competitive advantage over larger, VAT-registered rivals and reduce the time spent on paperwork.

In some countries you will also need to register with your local Chamber of Commerce. In the UK membership is voluntary. Chambers of Commerce are membership organisations for businesses of all sizes. They vary from city to city, but are a good source of business introductions. Most enable members to buy discounted services from trusted suppliers.

Case study
Keith Nicol, Costa Blanca TV

Keith Nicol has travelled the world as a professional filmmaker and has also presented TV programmes. He married a Spanish woman and now lives in Spain with his wife and son. He makes his living making wedding and corporate videos. ▶

Costa Blanca TV is very much Keith's brainchild. It's a web TV channel that will provide local news and views to the expat community in his area. Once established on the Costa Blanca, Keith plans to grow the business by franchising.

'At the moment, my business is virtual with my time being the biggest investment,' he explained. 'Once we are established and start to grow, I'll register as a company so that we are protected from some of the financial risk.'

Managing your company's finances is one of the more complex aspects of being an entrepreneur. For a more detailed guide to the entire process, see *Book-keeping and Accounts for Entrepreneurs* by Martin Quinn (Prentice Hall Business, 2009).

Frequently asked questions

Here are some typical questions asked by new entrepreneurs about the financial aspects of starting their businesses.

We're worried about bad debts and think that we should set up a limited company to protect ourselves. Do you agree?

There's no doubt that many people have come unstuck because of bad debt. However, rather than structure your business solely to protect you from the worst eventuality, set it up in a way that suits a more positive future. Then take all precautions to make sure you don't incur bad debts – for example, by taking customer deposits with orders to reduce your exposure.

My brother-in-law works for a firm of accountants and has offered to do our books, etc. for free. Is this a good idea?

Although it might cost you more, it is always good practice to keep some distance between your business and home lives. If you'd like to use your brother-in-law's services, do it via his firm so that the relationship remains professional.

My business will involve a lot of transactions in other countries. Should I go for a bank with a large overseas network?

I'd not make any assumptions that a large overseas network will make it easier for you to do foreign transactions. Meet the export advisers at a couple of banks and also talk to your local Chamber of Commerce. Then make your decision.

Another key decision you will face is finding the perfect business premises. The next chapter will address this.

Key points

→ You want to get the business structure right from the beginning; it can be costly to change later.

→ Don't hire the cheapest professional advisers. Use people who will become increasingly valuable to you as your enterprise grows.

→ Choose the structure that best suits your needs and future aspirations. Don't incorporate just to save a little tax. Focus on making money, not saving tax!

Next step

Reflect on *how* you work best as this will help you decide *where* you will work best. You almost certainly have a choice. Make the best decision for you.

_____

_____

_____

_____

Finding the perfect place – business premises

Chapter Six

A surprising number of people run their businesses from home. It is certainly convenient and low cost when compared with the alternatives. In fact, many businesses are started at home and remain based there for many years. There is no shame in operating a home-based business.

For many there is no choice. Family commitments, budget restraints and the convenience of a 30-second commute combine to make homeworking the best option for the long term.

> **A desk is a dangerous place from which to watch the world.** JOHN LE CARRÉ

Working from home: pros and cons

The economic benefits of working from home are obvious. You're not incurring any additional costs for rent or travel. Working in the back bedroom is very handy, particularly if you want to work odd hours to fit around childcare, for example.

Working from home is good if:

→ your customers do not expect to visit your place of work;

→ you have room to set aside for a dedicated office;

→ your business will not annoy or disturb your neighbours.

How to Start Your Own Business for Entrepreneurs

Working from home is bad if:

→ your business will quickly outgrow the space you have available;

→ you need to employ people and don't want them in your house;

→ you lack the self-discipline to ignore the TV/household chores/ garden and get on with the job.

Sir Richard Branson has always run his business from home. Although he now has a business empire, his core senior team work around him in what was, until a few years ago, the family home. To make more space, he bought and moved his family into the house next door.

Remember that the President of the USA and the Prime Minister of Great Britain both work from home!

How to work from home

If you're going to work from home, you need to make things as easy as possible for yourself and those you live with. A separate workspace is important, if only so you can concentrate without distraction and forget work when you're trying to relax. There are a number of things you can do to achieve this.

→ Invest in a dedicated business phone line or second 'work' mobile so you know whether you're being called by a customer or your mother. This also means you can opt not to take work calls in the evening without ignoring personal calls.

→ Buy yourself a decent desk and chair. You'll feel more professional if you avoid working at the dining room table.

→ Be disciplined about your time. Be either at work or at home. Don't let your multitasking bridge the gap.

→ If your clients do come to you at home (for instance, if you're a music teacher or therapist), keep tidy the parts of your home your visitors will use. Keep any clutter out of sight.

→ If you actually work from home, rather than at home, consider having your phone diverted to an answering service when you are out. Alternatively, make your mobile your work number and emphasise the fact that this gives your customers rapid access to you. This compensates for the less professional image a mobile number may create.

Top Tip

There are some stylish garden offices on the market today. They often don't need planning consent and enable you to keep work out of the house.

Case study
Alison Pitman, The Phone Voice,
www.thephonevoice.com

Alison Pitman has always worked in broadcast journalism and was taught how to read news bulletins and make voice news reports. She saw requests for voiceover presenters on a marketplace website and realised this was something she could easily do from home. With a two-year-old daughter this was vital.

The technology she needed to record voiceovers was just affordable and she was soon in business.

'I never meet my customers as the majority are based overseas,' she explained. 'All my client interactions take place online via email, which is convenient for everyone. They email me a script, I record it and then email back the audio file. I could not combine work and childcare any other way.'

How to make space at home to work

Before discounting the idea of working from home on grounds of space alone, consider the cost/merits of:

→ converting your garage or loft;

→ buying a 'home office building' for your garden;

→ refitting a spare bedroom with a fold-up bed to create a daytime work space.

Alternatives to working from home

If working from home is not for you, there are plenty of alternatives. Some of them are obvious, such as renting space in a business centre. Others are less obvious but should not be overlooked; these alternatives include the following.

→ Working at one of your customers' premises. This clearly commits them to you and may actually create opportunities as well as save costs. For example:

  – a graphic designer might be based at a printer's;

  – a haulier might base their truck at a customer's factory;

  – a bookkeeper might have space at a customer's offices.

→ Operating within a separate business. This can work well if your products or services complement those of your host. For example, a bag shop could be located within a ladies' fashion store or a café in an office complex.

→ A mobile business, where you take yourself and all your equipment in a van. This can work for carpet retailers, who take samples to the customers' homes rather than trying to attract them to a shop.

Lifestyle	High growth
This chapter will be particularly useful for you. Your priorities will be convenience and cost saving, as well, perhaps, as proximity to key customers.	Almost inevitably, you will be hiring people very early on, if not at start-up. This might make working at home difficult. For you, flexibility is vital, so your premises can expand as your team grows.

Case study
Silvano Milano, Park 'n' Trim

Silvano Milano was a gents' barber who wanted the freedom of working for himself. He tried renting a chair in a barber's shop in town but became restless. He preferred straightforward haircuts to elaborate styling and found he was losing out to more flamboyant rivals.

Then he had an idea. He bought a van and kitted it out as a barber's shop. He worked out a round that meant he spent half a day a week at ten different truck stops in his area. His theory was that truck drivers would welcome the chance to have a haircut during their compulsory rest breaks from driving. He was right and soon had a thriving business.

Finding premises

Sometimes it is simply not possible to start your business at home. Also it also might not be desirable. The premises you find for your new venture have to be affordable and add value to the enterprise.

There are several factors you need to consider when choosing business premises. The importance of each will vary, depending on what type of business you have, but all are significant.

Location

Where you site your business is important. This seems obvious, but you need to consider the following questions.

→ Will customers visit you and what impression will your location create?

→ How convenient is the location for you and any (future) employees?

→ Do you need to be near your competitors? (Important in retail.)

→ Are you close to suppliers or others it may be useful to have around?

→ Is the place bright and inspiring or dismal and depressing?

→ Remember, too, that you're going to spend a lot of time at your new place of work. It has to be somewhere you find appealing.

Tenure

When you start a business you're never totally sure what space you need. Retail is perhaps the only area where you have to commit to a place and stay there for some time, although even then, it's not unusual for shops to move to a more favourable location when the opportunity arises.

The key point here is to give yourself as much flexibility as possible. Most business premises are leasehold. Think about the following.

→ How long is the lease? Short leases can be cheap, but you'll have to move somewhere else at the end – perfect if you're anticipating rapid growth!

→ What breaks are there in the lease? These are the points at which you can move out without financial penalty. Note that if you sign a year-long lease, you are committed to paying a year's rent, even if you move out early.

→ Security of tenure. Be aware that most business tenancies are written in such a way that you do not have the same security of tenure as you would with a residential lease. Remember that breaks in leases work both ways. Your landlord can also ask you to move out if they need the space themselves.

→ Maintenance and repairs. You will inevitably be responsible for some of these costs. Be sure you understand what they are from the start.

> ### Top Tip
>
> A **tenancy** is the right to occupy land or buildings as provided by the terms of a lease or other agreement. A lease is the legal agreement by which you occupy land or buildings.

Rent

Unless you can afford to buy premises, you need to pay rent. Most business landlords ask for rent monthly or quarterly in advance. Some will ask for a deposit as well. When working out how much your premises will cost, bear in mind the following.

→ **VAT** Some landlords charge VAT on top of the rent and some don't. If you're not planning to register for VAT you won't be able to reclaim it.

→ **Business rates** In the UK, you will need to pay this to the local council on top of your rent. This is calculated on the 'rateable value' of the premises. Some councils subsidise the rates charge for small businesses. Always ask.

→ **Extras** Your rent may or may not include heat and light, broadband, parking and cleaning or any other extras.

Retail premises

If you are in retail, you need to consider some additional points when choosing a location. These include the following.

→ Do you want to be close to competitors or not? This can be good for restaurants as people often browse menus outside before making their choice. It can be bad if you're a laundrette, where you want to be the only place in the neighbourhood.

→ What do the neighbours do? A tattoo parlour may not prosper in a shopping centre and a chocolatier may not do well in the arty bohemian quarter of the city.

→ Who shops in the locality? What is the demographic profile of the local population? Can they afford what you're going to sell?

→ Footfall. The more you can attract passing trade, the less you will need to advertise to encourage people through the door.

Researching retail locations

Much of the success of a retail outlet is determined by its location. There is so much theory about how to find the perfect place for your shop. Big retailers will, for example, conduct detailed street surveys, look at demographic data for a shopping centre's catchment area and literally count how many people walk along the street at different times of the day.

Shop rents are largely dictated by location and footfall. Rent too good a location and you won't necessarily see sufficient additional turnover to cover the extra cost. Rent a poor location and you'll spend more than you save on advertising to tell people where you are.

One of the best ways to research retail locations is to visit them. This sounds obvious, but sitting in a coffee shop watching people walking along a street that you are considering can be time well spent. Your instinct will usually tell you as much as the shop landlord's promotional material.

Top Tip

Start your location research by people watching. Go there and see for yourself the kinds of people who walk past the shop you might rent. Do you think they'd stop and come in if you were there? Trust your instinct, it's usually right.

Top property tips

Before committing yourself to workspace, be sure to think about the following.

→ It is possible to rent just a desk in a business centre if that is all you need.
→ Consider sharing premises. If you work mainly for one customer, perhaps making components, it might be possible to base yourself on their site. You might also set up a 'shop within a shop' – for example, a conservatory showroom at a garden centre.

→ Never be afraid to negotiate. Your landlord probably needs you more than you need them.

Frequently asked questions

Finding the right place to work is important. Here are some typical concerns.

Working from home makes sense for my new business, but how can I avoid the temptation to spend the whole day in my pyjamas?

You need to be disciplined in having fixed working hours and a separate place to work and for some people it helps to dress for work as well, even if they are spending the day alone in the home office.

I have the opportunity to base my company at one of my clients' premises. However, I am worried that other clients might be put off if I am based within another company.

Basing yourself within a customer's premises means that you are pretty much assured of getting their business. Add to this the benefit of lower overheads and you can see why it can be a good idea. You need to invest some of that cost saving in making sure that you are seen as an independent business and not simply a department within your client's company. For example, you need a separate telephone line, some signage that announces your presence and ideally your own front door.

A good friend has offered us the opportunity to set up our shop within their shop. This means we can sell to their customers and, as our customer base grows, our customers will also buy from our friend. Our product ranges fit well together. The problem is that our friend is reluctant to put anything in writing – should we be worried about this?

I am sure your friend is offering to help you for all the right reasons. However, entering into any sort of business arrangement with a friend or, for that matter, with family is fraught with danger. When things are going well, everything will be fine, but if one or other of you starts to do significantly better than the other, tensions can arise. For your peace of mind, you need some kind of written agreement, ideally prepared by a solicitor. Then you both know exactly what you are committing to.

One alternative you may not have considered is taking over an existing business instead of starting from scratch. In the next chapter we'll look at the benefits and drawbacks of doing this.

Key points

→ Working from home can be great and is not second best.

→ You need to retain the flexibility to move premises as your business grows.

→ Don't be afraid to question the terms of a lease or to ask for the things you want included to be included.

→ Think very carefully before you sell the family home to buy a business that has accommodation, such as a pub. Better to rent a pub until you are totally confident it is the right business for you.

Next step

Before you commit to anything, particularly buying a business, make sure it looks profitable with only 75 per cent of the predicted sales. Plan for the worst and prepare for the best!

_____

_____

_____

_____

Starting up or taking over an existing enterprise

Chapter Seven

You might think it strange that a book about starting a business should suggest that you might take over one instead. The reality is, though, that sometimes taking over an existing business can be a better option.

You might also think that buying an existing business is beyond your reach. However, sometimes it costs less to take over an existing business than to start from scratch.

It is our choices . . . that show what we truly are, far more than our abilities. J. K. ROWLING

Case study

Howard Schultz, Starbucks,
http://starbucks.co.uk

When Howard Schultz joined Starbucks in the early 1980s, the company was already a highly respected local roaster and retailer of whole bean and ground coffees. A business trip to Italy opened his eyes to the rich tradition of the espresso beverage. Espresso drinks became an essential element of Schultz's vision. He purchased Starbucks with the support of local investors in 1987.

Since then he has grown a business, which was unknown outside Seattle, into a global brand. The success of Howard Schultz clearly demonstrates how much better it can be to buy an established business and grow it than to start from scratch.

Why take over an existing business?

The value of an existing business lies mostly within its:

→ customer base – specifically the likelihood that these customers will continue to buy;

→ reputation – increasingly measured by its Facebook 'likes' and Twitter followers;

→ potential – the market trends that mean future growth is likely;

→ intellectual property – which means others cannot copy what it does;

→ balance sheet – the things the business owns that will be included in the sale, including debtors.

A point to remember

If you leave a job to start up on your own and take customers with you, it's important to be able to demonstrate that you've not poached them or infringed your employment contract. Most contracts prohibit you canvassing your former employer's customers for a period of time after you've left. If they come with you, it must be because they've looked for and found you in your new guise.

Why do people sell their businesses?

To understand why you might be able to afford to buy a business you need to understand why people decide to sell. The motivation for selling will influence both the price and the time period over which you will have to pay. Buying a business is not as simple as buying a house or car.

People sell their business for one or more of a number of reasons. For example:

→ they want to retire or no longer have the good health to continue;

→ they're getting divorced and own the business with their ex;

→ they've lost interest or perhaps even lost the plot;

→ bad debts or management mistakes mean they have no cash;

→ the business has outgrown their ability to manage it effectively and become a burden.

The skill of buying a business is to work out the vendor's motivation and match your offer to both of your needs.

Top Tip

Sometimes it can be good simply to buy into a business rather than buy it outright. This means you retain the vendor's interest and participation. It also means you can buy the business a little at a time from the profits it generates.

Case study

Ben Dayman, Cornwall Cakes Ltd,
www.cornwallcakes.co.uk

Ben joined Cornwall Cakes in Bude as a pastry chef, having trained at North Devon College and after gaining chef experience at several hotels and restaurants in the area. He enjoyed working in a small successful team, watching the business grow as the reputation and popularity of their delicious desserts grew.

Then five years later, in 2009, owners Rob and Jo Bader seeking a change of direction and feeling they had taken the business as far as they could, put the business up for sale. Shortly after, also feeling his career needed fresh impetus Ben took advice and decided he'd like to buy the business. The owners were delighted and terms were agreed that worked for both Ben and the Baders.

'I knew the business inside and out and had a good rapport with the customer base,' said Ben. 'It seemed to make sense to buy the business I worked in and could steer forward with fresh ideas rather than find a few job or risk working for new owners who would operate the business differently.'

When is it better to start from scratch?

However appealing the idea of buying an existing business may seem, there are times when you'll be better to start from scratch. There are lots of benefits to creating a business from nothing. These include:

→ a marketplace with no preconceived ideas or expectations;

→ the opportunity to be new, fresh and different from competitors;

→ an ability to set your own pace, perhaps even starting part time.

However, don't fall for the myth that you will be starting a unique business. No business is truly unique. People need to compare your enterprise with others before they will see and understand the value you bring. Their innate suspicion of the unknown will make it difficult to market something really revolutionary and new.

Case study
Julie Begbie, Keepstakes,
www.keepstakes.co.uk

When Julie was on maternity leave with her second child, she started looking for business ideas. She wanted to work flexibly so that she could do the school run and be around when her children needed her. Julie also wanted a business she could be passionate about. She wanted to enjoy what she did as well as succeed.

She knew she liked making things and when a friend's baby received a tree with a handmade plaque, inspiration struck. The plan that led to the launch of Keepstakes grew and the business was born. Keepstakes makes personalised plaques that create unique, lasting gifts and keepsakes.

Julie did not rush into the business from day one. She chose instead to grow it slowly and steadily. When the time came that income from the business was enough to justify resigning from her job, she took the plunge and hasn't looked back since. Buying a business wasn't an option for Julie. She wanted to combine creating her business with the needs of her young children.

What do you want?

Before looking to see if a business is for sale, you have to work out what you're looking to buy. If you have a specific skill or interest, you need to focus there. If, on the other hand, your background is in general management, you want to keep a relatively open mind. Look for business models you understand, not just industry sectors where you have experience.

How to find a business for sale

Many businesses are advertised as being for sale, through classified advertising in magazines such as *Dalton's Weekly*, on specialist websites and through specialist brokers called 'business transfer agents'. Other places to look include:

→ accountants, who will often discreetly market a client's business;

→ your employer, who might be receptive to you buying out all or a part of their organisation;

→ people within your existing business network who might know someone who's thinking of selling.

Once you have identified a business that might be for sale, you can investigate it online to find out more about the owners and why they might be selling. There is nothing sinister about this as all the information you will glean is freely available. Try the following.

→ If it's a limited company, you can obtain financial performance, shareholder and director information online. You often have to pay for this, although public libraries often have subscriptions you can use to access the data you need.

→ 'Like' the company on Facebook and follow on Twitter to see what they are saying about themselves.

→ Check out user review websites (e.g., Trip Advisor) to see what customers say. In particular, look for trends, good or bad.

→ Set up a Google Alert on the company or product name. This means you'll receive an email whenever Google detects a new reference to the words you have registered for alerts.

Make an offer

Often the best way to buy a business is to find one you think may meet your needs and suggest a buyout to the owner. It can be very flattering to receive an approach from a prospective buyer, so don't worry about upsetting the owner. It's rather like receiving an email from a headhunter at work; you may be happy in your job, but it's nice to be offered an alternative.

Signs to look out for include the following.

→ **Complacency** This is best illustrated in the retail sector, but it is equally true of all business types. The shop owner that has become complacent might:
  - not keep window displays up to date;
  - be slow to repair damage, such as broken lights;
  - have demotivated staff;
  - carry old, dusty stock;
  - be slow to serve you and be unenthusiastic.

→ **Not keeping up** This often means that any competitive advantage is eroded as interest may be waning. Signs that a business is slipping behind can include:
  - lack of recent investment in vehicles and technology;
  - slow response to changing market trends;
  - lapsed membership of trade and business networks;
  - reduction in marketing expenditure.

→ **Running out of money** This is indicated by:
  - County Court judgments;
  - redundancies;
  - suppliers beginning to talk/rumour.

→ **Personal problems** Divorce is not the only personal problem that can mean a business owner might be willing to sell. Others include:

- illness or death of a partner/shareholder;
- boardroom arguments/partner disagreements;
- prosecution for a serious offence;
- an ambition to do something new.

> **Top Tip**
>
> By far the best way to make a cold approach is by email. Make sure, though, you have the individual's personal email address. An address such as **info@thebusiness.co.uk** is unlikely to be opened by the business owner. Do some research first. **www.linkedin.com** is a good place to start.

How to buy a business, step by step

You cannot buy a business without professional help. Your accountant and solicitor are crucial in making sure you don't make a big mistake. They will inevitably lack your enthusiasm for the deal you're trying to do. They will also encourage you to explore aspects of the purchase that you might otherwise overlook.

What you need to remember is that professional advisers have dealt with many similar transactions. You will be emotionally involved and have bought the dream. They simply look at the stark facts and guide you through the following steps.

Valuing a business

Working out what a business is worth is not as straightforward as valuing a house. This is because there is much more to consider than simply the asset value of the enterprise. Value is largely dependent on the enterprise's future potential to generate profit.

A major part of that future potential will depend on your ability to manage the business. If you know the sector, are well connected and have the skills to build up what you are buying, the value to you is greater than if you do not. Large organisations often buy (and sell) a business to improve their distribution or to align themselves with a wider corporate vision. This can also distort a business' value.

Most people selling a business will make the running and suggest a price. You and your advisers need to explore:

→ assets such as premises, plant and equipment;

→ past trading performance;

→ future trading projections;

→ customer 'stickiness' (volume of repeat business);

→ current accounts (debtors, creditors, work in progress);

→ any patents or trade agreements that maintain exclusivity;

→ motivation for selling (the more the vendor wants to sell, the better your bargaining position).

You also need to be confident that you fully appreciate what's happening in the business' marketplace.

→ Is demand growing or declining?

→ Is market share increasing or decreasing? (Remember that if the market is growing at 10 per cent per annum and the business is growing at 5 per cent per annum, it is actually losing market share.)

→ Are competitors gaining ground?

→ What impact will planned or predicted legislation have?

→ What innovation is there within the business and within the marketplace?

Top Tip

Your accountant will be able to help you with a process called 'due diligence'. This is a professional look into the company's finances, value and exposure to risk.

Lifestyle	High growth
Due diligence can be quite 'light touch' if you are buying a lifestyle business. It's as much about the people as the performance of the enterprise.	Thorough due diligence where the potential for growth is high is a must. For one thing, the stakes are higher and, for another, the process should form an integral part of the takeover negotiations.

Doing the deal

Contrary to what you might believe, few businesses actually sell for the asking price in one cash sum. That's because savvy buyers negotiate a deal that enables them to spread their risk and, as far as possible, lets the business they're buying generate the money needed to pay off the former owner. Typical types of company transaction include:

→ earn out – where the vendor remains with the business and the money they actually get is linked directly to trading performance;

→ earn in – where you pay an agreed price from your share of the profits generated (this is how new partners often acquire a share of the firm they've joined);

→ various performance-related deals – where the vendor leaves but is paid sums that are linked to company performance over a period of years;

→ staged purchase – where you might buy a trading company and have an agreed deal to buy the premises it occupies later.

The vendor will want to minimise their tax liability on the sale proceeds. There can be a financial incentive for them to sell the business in stages over a number of years.

Top Tip

Have your accountant work out the likely tax position of the owner of the business you are buying. Then you're more likely to offer them a deal that is better for both of you. Do not assume that your vendor has taken similar advice. Many don't!

How to Start Your Own Business for Entrepreneurs

Due diligence

This is where your advisers (usually your accountant and solicitor) really earn their fees. As well as helping you to structure and perhaps negotiate the deal, they will look at:

→ the management accounts, to determine true profitability (many owner-managers take income from the business in several ways and so the business might be more profitable than it appears at first glance);

→ contracts with customers and suppliers, to find problems and liabilities;

→ employee contracts, staff rights and liabilities that might transfer to you – for example, pension rights and profit-sharing schemes;

→ any current legal disputes that might impact the deal;

→ environmental commitments and risk;

→ infrastructure issues, such as IT systems.

The most important element of all to bear in mind when buying a business is to be totally confident that you can make it work. It is almost always better to walk away from a deal you don't feel comfortable with than to risk burdening yourself with a business that will cause you problems. This is quite different from starting up from scratch, where you should be encouraged to talk to prospective customers and experiment, rather than spend too much time trying to work out what's going to succeed for you.

Top Tip

Increasingly, teams are moving out from the public sector to join commercial businesses and social enterprises. Where you are likely to acquire employees under Transfer of Undertakings (Protection of Employment) Regulations (TUPE) you need to fully understand the liabilities this may bring. These particularly apply to pension and possible future redundancy payments. These liabilities need to be factored into the transfer deal.

Frequently asked questions

The following are some of the types of questions asked about taking over a business.

I've been talking with the family of a garage owner who is now in prison for growing cannabis at his business premises. Do you think the owner's chequered history will harm my chances of rebuilding the business if I buy it?

There's no doubt that reputation can work both ways. That said, if the owner is in prison, he's not going to get as good a price for the garage as he would if he'd not suddenly abandoned it when arrested. Drive a hard bargain, with compassion, and don't try to conceal the reason for the takeover. Notoriety can be a selling point.

There's a derelict shop in my market town that I think would make a wonderful café. It's just come onto the market. It's a wreck but would be stunning if restored sensitively. What do you think?

Which do you want to do most? Open a café or restore an old building? Both can be profitable if tackled separately. Both can fail if tackled together. Only embark on this kind of project if you have more money than you think you'll need. For one thing, the restoration might well go over budget and, for another, your café might not open as soon as you might hope.

I'm negotiating to take over a flagging print business. The owner is past retiring age and is losing customers, but he won't accept anything like a realistic price. How can I encourage him to see sense?

You probably can't. He's worked on his own for maybe 30 years and may never have taken advice from anyone. Walk away but stay friends. Keep your eye on things because, almost inevitably, the decline will continue. If you do end up getting a deal some time in the future, be kind to him. Don't say, 'If we'd done this ages ago you'd have got a better price.'

How to Start Your Own Business for Entrepreneurs

Key points

→ Don't assume that you have to start a business from scratch. Sometimes you can buy something that's up and running.

→ If you want to buy a business, spread the word. It might encourage someone to surprise you!

→ Remember that your business might also have a greater value to someone else than to yourself. Be receptive to offers, even if you decide not to accept them.

Next step

Check the plan you're writing right now. To what extent is it a work of fiction? Remember that while a bold vision is important, writing down the impossible will not make it happen

_____

_____

_____

_____

Planning to succeed

Part Two

How to write a convincing plan

Chapter Eight

The business adage, 'If you fail to plan you are planning to fail', is perhaps one of the truest pieces of advice anyone can give you, but that does not mean a business plan has to be a large or complex document. Nobody measures a business plan by its length. Keep it short and to the point. You can always add detailed appendices for those who need them.

The best business plan is the one you write yourself that is short, simple to understand and, above all else, believably illustrates how you plan to realise your personal vision.

Traditionally, advisers would suggest that your business plan should be written to appeal to your bank manager. Some might even suggest they write the plan for you. However badly you write, your plan will carry more weight if you have written it, understand it and, most of all, believe it to be deliverable. Bank managers can quickly see through a plan written simply to win their support.

A potential lender or investor in your venture will learn all they need about you, your business ambition and ability in the first ten minutes of conversation with you. The most ambitious, complicated, cleverly written business plan in the world will not sway someone whose first impression is that you haven't got what it takes to succeed.

Conversely, a concise, explicit plan that shows you have researched your idea, have thought about what you are going to do and understand the basic rules of business is more than enough, providing that you also are passionate, persuasive and convincing face to face.

 Life is what happens to you while you're busy making other plans. JOHN LENNON

What does a good business plan contain?

The best business plans are often the shortest. They summarise in two or three pages the opportunity, the challenges and the resources needed to make it happen. While the business plan is a serious document, there is nothing wrong with illustrating it with pictures and graphs. The objective is to communicate clearly and quickly.

How to Start Your Own Business for Entrepreneurs

The narrative is supported by a single-page spreadsheet that summarises cash flow for the first 12 months. This shows what money is needed to establish the business and, ideally, also charts the initial signs of profitability.

Even if you are not confident about writing a business plan yourself, it's a good idea to try, then simply ask someone else to help work on it further. Your business plan has to be exactly that: your business plan. Only you know what you want to achieve and you need to explore and express that in your own words. Once you have done this, you can ask someone to tidy up the document and correct any spelling and grammatical errors.

Of course, the plan also has to be appropriate to the scale of the business you are starting. If you are going to work from home as a tradesperson or consultant, becoming effectively self-employed, you need a less detailed plan than if you are planning with your colleagues to buy out part of your employer's company.

However much detail your plan actually requires, it is always good practise to begin with a simple two-page summary. For some that will be all they need; for others it merely sets the scene for the detail that will follow.

Top Tip

If you're starting a simple business, you only need a simple plan.

Case study
Jeff Clark, Admiral Design and Print,
www.admiraldesignandprint.co.uk

When Jeff Clark reached 40, his wife told him it was time to plan the second half of his career. There were, she said, 20 years left to realise their ambition.

The couple decided to start a business together and began to look around. They wanted a business they could relate to, that met a clear market need. They also wanted a business that would allow them to build and maintain relationships with other businesspeople, rather than provide a one-off service.

▶

Their research and backgrounds led them to buy an existing printing company. New to print, they kept on the existing employees and set out to grow their new enterprise. Jeff's business plan acknowledged the fact that the print industry was in decline, but identified, by introducing design, focusing on service and adding real value to each job, they could buck the downward industry trend.

After six years of trading, turnover has more than doubled and profits have grown. 'In 2010 we acquired another print business. Admiral Charity Cards now runs alongside Admiral Design and Print, further doubling turnover and increasing profit.'

Why a short business plan is better than a long plan

It is very tempting to write a traditional and comprehensive business plan, particularly if you are following one of the many templates provided by the banks and business support agencies.

Writing a short plan has several benefits. For example:

→ it will be easier to read and remember;

→ it will force you to be focused and specific;

→ busy people – for example, bank managers and business angels – will be able to make a rapid assessment and quickly spot the pertinent facts.

Remember that it can take longer to write a short business plan than a long one. That's because the process makes you think. Thinking is good!

Lifestyle	*High growth*
Your plan is largely for your own peace of mind. Your investment may be modest and the risk fairly low. Short and sweet is what will work best.	Here the stakes are higher. Most high-growth businesses need external investment. This means a more extensive business plan with professionally prepared financial projections.

Who needs to read your plan and why?

Your business plan should be your business route map, summarising the journey and identifying when you need to refuel and who you need to pick up along the way. A good business plan is one that you choose to keep close and handy, rather than filed away in a drawer.

Initially your business plan's function is convincing you and perhaps those close to you that the enterprise you are proposing will succeed. In fact, it is often a good idea to let your life partner critique your business plan before you release it for wider circulation. They won't necessarily understand the business you are about to begin, but they will understand you and challenge you if they think you are being unrealistic or too bold.

Other people who might need to see your business plan include the following.

→ **Bank manager** Even if you are not planning to borrow money, the manager of your business bank account will want to see a business plan. You need to be enthusiastic about your enterprise. Encourage your bank manager to give critical feedback.

→ **Landlord** Particularly if you are starting a retail business, it is important for the landlord to know that they are letting to a business that will become successful. If you were a landlord with a prime retail location to let, you would need convincing to let it to a new business rather than to a more established operator.

→ **Investor** Business investors come in all shapes and sizes. One thing that unites them all is that they will want to see and question a credible business plan before parting with any money.

→ **Key employees** Although most new UK businesses do not employ staff, some do. If you are recruiting a key person whose commitment is vital to your success, it makes sense for them to read, understand and believe in your business plan.

Case study

Waqas Baggia,
www.kreativeiron.com

Waqas Baggia set up Kreative Iron, a graphics and web business, in the industrial West Midlands. Despite having an MBA, he still decided to use business planning software to help him put together a plan for his new company.

'I used Business Plan Pro, which saved numerous hours formatting the plan and producing the financial projections,' he said. 'I particularly liked the built-in checks that warned me if my projections were not looking credible or viable.'

Waqas used software to save time and check that what he was proposing was viable. His business journey has been a little rocky since he started, but he remains confident about the future. He represented the UK at the G20 Young Entrepreneur Summit in Toronto in 2010. (Business Plan Pro is a product of Palo Alto Software **www.paloalto.com/uk**).

How to write a business plan, step by step

Here are the essential components of a successful business plan and a suggested format for each, with examples.

Your vision

This is one paragraph that captures exactly what your business is going to achieve and why it is important.

Example: 'Blue Sky Home Care will provide sensitive, flexible and responsible care services that enable older people to remain in their homes rather than move to residential care.'

It is important that the vision statement promises clear benefits to the customer group as well as to you as the entrepreneur. Your business needs to meet a recognised need, as well as realising your ambition.

Why you?

Next, you need a paragraph that explains why you are uniquely placed to make this business work.

Example: 'After five years of commissioning domiciliary care for older people in my job at the Council, I know exactly what service commissioners, service users and their families expect. Having audited service suppliers for three of those years I also know what makes both the difference and a profit.'

Outline why your recent experience, knowledge and network clearly demonstrate that you are the one person who can make this happen.

Market share

How big is the market you are aiming at, where is it and how much are you planning to take?

Example: 'There are currently 60,000 elderly people receiving domiciliary care in my borough. Demographics suggest that this number will grow by 10 per cent a year over the next 10 years. We plan to grow to deliver 10 per cent of that market within 3 years.'

You do not need to quote detailed statistics or data to prove that you know your market. Many people make the mistake of duplicating pages of facts and figures. All you need are those that matter.

Products/services

Now explain exactly what you will be selling and to whom.

Example: 'We will offer three levels of care: bronze, silver and gold. If the Council is funding the bronze level, a family will be encouraged to pay the difference to upgrade their aged relative. Silver and gold levels will include extra services such as ironing, shopping and cooking.'

Profit

Show in summary how your selling price is calculated. A one-page spreadsheet projecting your first year's cash flow is also needed, detailing how your overhead costs will be covered and identifying any need for borrowing.

Example: 'The attached spreadsheet shows how we have calculated that our services will be charged on an all-inclusive, weekly basis. Profitability will be higher on the silver and highest at the gold service level.'

This information needs to be backed up with service prices, ideally compared with competitor pricing, to show where you will fit in your marketplace.

People

Describe briefly the skills you need and how you will recruit, develop and retain the best people for the job.

Example: 'I am a qualified general manager. We will build our own bank of care and domestic workers on flexible contracts to meet operational needs. We have an arrangement with the local college to audit and develop our people's skills.'

Will you subcontract, use agency staff or employ people? Show you've considered the risk as well as the opportunity.

Exit strategy

Although you might not see yourself selling the business in the foreseeable future, it's important to show that you've thought about what happens when you've had enough.

Example: 'My daughter is training as a social worker and, after gaining a few years' work experience, plans to join me in the business and then take over from me when I retire in ten years' time.'

Frequently asked questions

The following are some typical questions that new entrepreneurs may ask about business plans after reading this book.

I need to borrow money to start my business and a consultant has suggested I would do better with a professionally written plan than one I had prepared myself. What do you think?

A slick business plan written for you may well impress a business angel or funder. The problems will arise when they start asking questions and expect you to know the answers. A business plan, however well written, cannot create a business without an entrepreneur. Your plan needs to fit you as much as it does your business.

You suggest that the vision statement for my business should explain how the business can help other people, but actually deep down all I really want to do is help myself. Is this really a problem?

Every business needs customers and those customers need to see clearly that the value they are gaining by dealing with you is greater than the cost. You need to be convinced that this is what you are doing before you can convince them.

I have read this chapter and I know what you're suggesting but I am still finding it difficult to get started. Can you help?

It could be that your business idea is not yet fully formed in your mind. If that is the case, perhaps you need to do more research. If, however, the problem is simply a lack of inspiration, take a look around on the internet and see how other businesses describe themselves. If you look hard enough you will probably find some sample business plans you can download and use to get you started.

Key points

→ The best business plans are short and to the point. Less can mean more.

→ Write the plan with the reader in mind.

→ Remember that the benefits to your customers have to be worth more than they will cost.

Next step

Take a second look at your cash flow projections. The figures now work, but is it still the business you first envisaged? If not, you might need to reconsider.

_____

_____

_____

_____

Where to find the money you need

Chapter Nine

Every new business needs funding to some extent. Even if you are simply going to sell your time, work from home and use the family car to get to clients' premises, you will have a cash flow gap to fill.

It is unusual to be paid in advance for the work that you do. If you supply businesses you may have to wait 30, 60 and often 90 days before receiving payment. While you are waiting to be paid, you still have your day-to-day living expenses to cover, the car to run and the mortgage. You probably also have some specific business expenses to find money for as well.

You also need to have some rainy day money put to one side for the inevitable month when things go wrong or sales are slow. Just as a financial adviser will encourage you to have three months' salary in the bank to act as a buffer, as an entrepreneur you need room to manoeuvre, too.

It is a sobering fact to learn that the single biggest cause of business failure is running out of money. Conversely, keeping on top of cash flow and making sure you focus on the most profitable work you do is the biggest cause of business success.

> **A bank is a place that will lend you money if you can prove that you don't need it.** BOB HOPE

Working out how much money you need

Calculating how much money you need to establish and grow your business for the first year or two is rather like guessing the length of that proverbial piece of string. There are so many variable factors to consider that it is easy to miscalculate. It is easy to fool yourself into thinking that you need less than you really do.

Top Tip

Don't kid yourself when working out your business and personal budget. It's better to err on the side of caution and overestimate rather than underestimate how much money you will need. If you can, always have enough in the bank to fund yourself for three months.

Here are some factors you will need to take into account when calculating how much money you require to start your business.

→ **Living expenses** It may well be several months before your new business is able to pay you. You need to factor your living expenses for the first few months into your start-up cost calculations.

Top Tip

It can be harder than you think to work out how much money you need each month to cover your living expenses. There's a free useful online calculator at **www.thisismoney.co.uk/household-budget-calculator**.

→ **Equipment** Depending on the business you are starting, you will need to equip yourself. This may be as simple as buying a new computer or as involved as fitting out a shop or factory unit.

→ **Stock and materials** If you are going to make or retail anything, you will need to carry stock and buy raw materials. For example, if you are opening a restaurant you may need to furnish and decorate it or fit or perhaps modernise the kitchen. You will also need to stock the larder and wine cellar. And don't forget crockery, cutlery, glasses and table linen. Make a list of what you need and work out what it's going to cost.

→ **Marketing** You will need to launch your new business and promote it to prospective customers. Even if you are going to promote your business purely by word of mouth, you will need a website and business stationery. Invite a couple of marketing companies to suggest a launch campaign and budget. You don't have to accept their offers but it's useful to know what marketing can cost.

→ **Premises** You will probably rent premises to start with and will find that many landlords look for several months' rent in advance. You may also have to pay legal fees to set up a lease. Even if you decide to work from home, you may have to make some alterations and will certainly need additional insurance. Again, make a list.

→ **Money** Borrowing money costs money. In your calculations, allow for bank fees and charges incurred in setting up an overdraft or bank loan. Your bank will often ask to take a second charge over your home. This means they have your house as security should you default on repayments. You may have to pay a valuation fee as well. Bank fees are often added to the loan, but they need to be allowed for all the same.

> **Top Tip**
>
> The VAT you pay on the things you purchase to set up your business can be claimed back on your first VAT return, even if you have not registered for VAT when you start. There is a time limit for this. For details, check at **www.hmrc.gov.uk**

Why too much is better than too little

There is no such thing as having too much money to start a business. Money gives you choice and flexibility. Too little money and you will find yourself becoming anxious about cash flow. The one thing you need to minimise when you start a business is your anxiety!

When you produce your cash flow forecast you will make assumptions about when people will pay you. Picture a spreadsheet with each vertical column representing one month. The top half of the spreadsheet will show your income and the bottom half your expenditure. Usually that is the way these statements are prepared. The very top line shows the opening balance in the bank and the very bottom line the closing balance.

You don't need much imagination to appreciate that if your income is delayed by one month, you have two months' running costs to cover instead of just one. This could have a dramatic effect on your bank balance. In fact, it is just this effect that leads rapidly growing businesses to run out of money. It is the time gap between incurring costs and banking the revenue those costs generate. This is why managing cash flow is so important.

How to Start Your Own Business for Entrepreneurs

This table assumes people pay promptly, within one month:

Month	1	2	3	4
Opening balance	£1,000	£500	£1,000	£1,500
Sales income	£0	£1,000	£1,000	£1,000
Purchases	£500	£500	£500	£500
Closing balance	£500	£1,000	£1,500	£2,000

This table assumes people pay late, in three months:

Month	1	2	3	4
Opening balance	£1,000	£500	£0	£500
Sales income	£0	£0	£1,000	£1,000
Purchases	£500	£500	£500	£500
Closing balance	£500	£0	£500	£1,000

You can see that in the second table you find yourself with no money in the bank at the end of month two. This very simple example shows how a small shift in payment date can have a major impact on your cash flow.

Clearly one way round this is to pay your suppliers late as well. Unfortunately, suppliers are unlikely to give a new company credit and may even demand cash with orders for the first few months. This widens the gap further.

Never be ashamed of the fact that you're starting a new business. Many people will understand how important cash flow is and, if asked, will pay their invoices in part or in full before they are due. This helps cash flow and enables you to build a cash buffer.

How to self-fund your new business

Even if interest rates are low, borrowing money can be expensive. Furthermore, most banks will look for personal guarantees and possibly want to take a second charge over your property. This means that should your business fail, you will have to find the money to repay the bank.

It makes sense, therefore, to borrow as little as you can, as cheaply as you can. Whichever way you look at it, if you have borrowed from the bank you are the one taking the financial risk. Here are some ways you can fund your business yourself.

Increase the mortgage

By far the cheapest source of business finance is to increase the mortgage on your home. Clearly you should not do this without taking professional advice. Many business starters negotiate a flexible or offset mortgage deal. This enables them to draw out money and repay it without incurring costly fees or penalties.

The business benefit of borrowing against the value of your home is that you can spread the repayment over several years. What's more, if you have a flexible mortgage, together with plenty of self-discipline, you can take a repayment holiday if necessary. This is where you stop repayments for a few months, with the consent of your lender.

Ask customers to pay in advance

It is not unusual for a customer to agree to staged payments to help your cash flow. Customers have every incentive to see your business grow, as it widens their choice of supplier. In some cases customers may even be prepared to make significant prepayments to get you started. This has the added benefit of guaranteeing their commitment to buy from you. Your bank, in particular, will be encouraged by this.

Ask suppliers to extend credit

Your suppliers will be keen to support you as a new customer. They may be willing to help by allowing you extended credit to ease your cash flow in the early months. It is always worth asking them this. However, if they do allow you to pay late, make sure you pay promptly. You do not want the concession withdrawn.

Gilbert's strategy for finding the money he needs may not be ideal.

Case study

James Robinson, The Discounter,
www.thediscounter.co.uk

Already a self-employed personal trainer in his early twenties, James knew that he wanted to build a business that would not be restricted by the number of hours he could work each day. He lived in a town with a high population of low-paid migrant workers and knew they found shopping in many high street shops too expensive. He started trading end-of-range clothing on eBay, buying recognised brands from specialist wholesalers.

Soon his new business started to take off. He kept his personal training clients as this meant he didn't need to take income from his new venture. His mother agreed to take on packing and posting and soon her house was filled with stock.

Now The Discounter is an established online retailer with a growing reputation. James plans to invest his profit in opening his first shop in the town where he lives. At every step of the way, James has funded his business expansion organically. As he opens more stores, he will inevitably need to borrow, but he will never be as financially exposed as many of his high street rivals.

Why do you need investors?

Even if you have the money to self-fund, it doesn't necessarily mean that you are the most appropriate person to invest. The earlier points about seeking working capital from customers and suppliers can often make more sense.

Most businesses need investment as they grow. This is because a growing business needs to spend money on people, products and premises before the revenue from those investments starts to flow.

There is an important distinction between bank funding and external investment. Bank lending tends to be short term and overdrafts, in particular, can be called in at a moment's notice – as the small print inevitably states.

Lifestyle	High growth
If you have a lifestyle business, you might be able to fund it yourself. However, it can be a useful discipline to seek external funding, too. If nothing else, if people are willing to invest it shows you're being taken seriously.	Funding growth can be a constant struggle. You need investment to maintain growth, yet, understandably, do not want to lose too much equity. Balancing this is just one of the challenges unique to the high-growth venture.

Where to look for outside investors

Hermann Hauser, founder of Acorn Computers and now a business investor, says that the first places you should look for funding are 'family and fools'. This seemingly harsh statement is totally true. That's because any investor will need to believe in you first and your business proposition second. Your family and friends know you best, so they will naturally have faith in your ability to deliver.

Fools are another matter. While there are people around foolish enough to invest in almost anything, that is not what Hauser meant. His point was more that people who believe in you are likely to make what, to the outsider, can seem like a foolish investment.

Whoever you recruit to invest in your business, they will want a return on their investment. Even your mother will expect a payback – even if it's just the satisfaction of seeing you succeed.

There are more places to look for investment than it first appears. All will demand a good business plan and a strong pitch, but each will make different demands on you in terms of return on their investment.

Case study
Anthony Davison, BigBarn CIC,
www.bigbarn.co.uk

Fifth-generation farmer Anthony Davison set up BigBarn to make it easier for consumers to buy their food from local farmers and producers. With 6,700 member producers and a growing following of consumers eager to buy their food direct, Anthony raised £12,000 to upgrade his website and marketing.

He could have gone to the bank for a loan, but chose instead to enable his customers to invest. Collectively, the £12,000 would buy investors a 4 per cent stake in the business. The offer was placed with Crowdcube, a crowdsourcing web platform, and, within 3 months, 58 people had invested and the target was reached.

For more information on Crowdcube go to **www.crowdcube.com**.

Enterprise Finance Guarantee Scheme

Your local business support agency can help you to apply for a loan under this UK government scheme. It is designed for situations where a bank is happy to lend you the money, but there's not enough security to cover the loan. For example, you may want to borrow £10,000 but your partner (who jointly owns the family home) is not prepared to allow the bank to take a charge over it. The government guarantees 75 per cent of the loan and you pay what is, in effect, an insurance premium of 2 per cent p.a. This is added to the loan to cover the risk. See **www.bis. gov.uk/policies/enterprise-and-business-support/access-to-finance/enterprise-finance-guarantee**.

Good points:	Bad points:
enables you to borrow when the banks would otherwise say no	can be costly to set up, although charges are usually added to the loan
the lender does not take any shares in your business	can take a long time to set up

Grants

Sometimes you can obtain a grant to help cover the cost of setting up your business. The availability of grant funding and the eligibility criteria to receive grants are constantly changing.

Grants are most often focused on funding:

→ business establishments in deprived communities or run by people battling with disadvantage;

→ capital equipment needed to compete in a regionally strategic business sector;

→ training and development for you and those you employ;

→ environmental good practice;

→ social enterprise.

Government business advisers can advise you on grants. There are also a number of online databases you can search – see **www.fundingcentral.org.uk**

Good points:	Bad points:
enable you to fund things you otherwise could not afford	the application process can be long and complicated
grants do not have to be paid back	it can be tempting to do something because there's a grant available

Prince's Trust, www.princes-trust.org.uk

Founded and led by Prince Charles, this charity provides a range of support to disadvantaged young people (aged under 30).

For budding entrepreneurs, it provides:

→ free business advice and start-up training;

→ unsecured business loans at preferential rates;

→ small grants;

→ two years' free business mentoring by an established volunteer business mentor.

Good points:	Bad points:
offers sound advice and practical support to those who need it most	the Trust has a finite budget and can't support as many as it would like
being supported by the Trust can win you positive publicity	a lot hangs on the relationship you forge with your mentor

Business angels

Business angels are the funders most people dream of meeting. Popular TV programmes show entrepreneurs pitching to panels of investors. Business angels are different from other lenders in that they:

→ invest in the potential as much as what's already been achieved;

→ take a share in the business in return for their investment;

→ often get personally involved, helping you to build the business.

Business angels can be hard to find and difficult to approach. Most only invest in business sectors they understand. Many join networks such as **www.nban.co.uk**, but many more work alone, relying on accountants and other intermediaries to broker introductions.

Good points:	Bad points:
their investment and support can enable you to grow a business quickly	they usually take a significant equity stake in your business, so it's no longer all yours
you can end up rich	angels usually want to sell as soon as they can be sure of getting a good return

Top Tip

If you give up too much equity in order to secure investment, you may find yourself no longer in control of your business.

Frequently asked questions

Here are some questions frequently asked by new entrepreneurs about finding funding for their businesses.

I've got a well-paid job, young family, large mortgage and modest savings. I hate my job and want to work for myself. How can I borrow enough to start the business and pay the bills for the first six months?

You probably can't! Consider starting your business part time and negotiate a gradual reduction in the hours you work for your employer. Many would prefer a phased transition to a shock resignation. Minimise your personal risk by taking it one step at a time.

My dad has offered to lend me the money I need, but I feel a little embarrassed taking it and feel I'm somehow taking advantage of him. What should I do?

I'd take him along to a solicitor or accountant and draw up a proper agreement between you. Is it a loan or a gift? Do you want him to have a share of the business? What's going to be the most tax-efficient option for him? Document the deal and treat it as you would an investment by a stranger.

I'm about to open a themed restaurant and have been offered a grant if I set the business up in a neighbourhood undergoing regeneration. What would you do?
I'd open the business where I thought the most customers would patronise it. Grants can reduce costs, but being in the wrong location can make even the best-funded business fail. Consider the risks and follow your instinct.

If doing all this sounds like a lonely proposition, take heart – there is an ample supply of advisers and mentors available, as you will find in the next chapter.

Key points

→ It's better to have too much money than too little. Be realistic when working out start-up costs. You're only fooling yourself if you underestimate your need.

→ Success is all about profit. The more profitable your business, the more cash it will generate to fund growth.

→ Cash flow is king. Never let doing the work distract you from getting paid on time.

Next step

Remember that your life partner, best friend or even your mum will also be valuable advisers. They probably won't understand your business challenge, but they will understand you!

_____

_____

_____

_____

Advisers and mentors and why they're important

Chapter Ten

It is human nature not to seek help. People sometimes see it as an admission of weakness to ask for advice. They choose to battle on alone instead. In business, as well as in other aspects of life, the opposite is more usually the case. It can take huge strength to ask for help when you're beginning to flounder. The majority of the most successful entrepreneurs you meet will tell you they readily sought advice at critical points in their business career. However, it's important to get advice from the right people.

Never trust the advice of a man in difficulties.

AESOP

> **Top Tip**
>
> The UK Government's Business Link website is a constantly updated, valuable source of impartial, independent business information. Check it out at **www.businesslink.gov.uk**

What does a good business adviser really do?

Research shows that when entrepreneurs do look for advice, the first place they visit is their local café or bar. Friends and acquaintances are the people most likely to be asked to offer inspiration to the new entrepreneur facing a challenge.

Sometimes those people have the answers, particularly if they happen to run their own businesses and have faced similar obstacles themselves. However, if they do not have business experience but see themselves as experts, their advice can be misleading and potentially catastrophic. Young businesses, rather like babies, are very vulnerable and need lots of loving care.

The best business advice is given by people who:

→ have experienced or solved the problem you are facing;

→ are independent and unbiased by any personal or commercial motive;

→ challenge you to think differently;

→ will stay with you until the issue has been resolved;

→ have integrity, enthusiasm and a genuine interest in your success.

These people may be professional business advisers working for a business support organisation. They may also be volunteer business mentors (see **www.mentorsme.co.uk**). Finally, they may be specialists within an accountancy practice or other professional business service providers.

Being experienced and knowledgeable is not enough. Choose advisers who you can relate to and respect as well. A good adviser gets in close to the business and needs your confidence and trust to be effective.

Case study
Ed Bodiam, SME Advice,
http://smeadvice.co.uk

A career providing technology and strategy solutions to small and medium-sized companies gave Ed Bodiam a valuable insight into the challenges business owners face. He set up SME Advice in 2008 to provide 'virtual Board members' to his clients as they face change or go for growth.

'I don't try to help unless I know I can and I only help owners who want to grow their businesses,' he told me, going on to explain how some people have quite jaundiced opinions of consultants in general. Ed's advice is to look at what a consultant has achieved with others before taking at face value what they claim to be able to do for you.

'Much of the value of using an external consultant as a sounding board and mentor is in the discipline it imposes on you,' he explained. 'You are far less likely to let things slip.'

SME Advice is a part of the Future Reliance Group (**www.futurereliancegroup. com**), of which Ed is CEO.

Just why is an outside opinion so important?

Every good entrepreneur lives and breathes their business, certainly for the first year or so. They take an almost obsessive interest in every aspect of the organisation they are building. This determination to succeed is positive, but the downside is that they may lose objectivity. You can become so close to the trees that you forget you're in a wood.

The input and opinion of people from outside the business can help you remain objective. All you have to do is invite comment and listen to what is said. You do not have to act on everything you hear, but it is important to take on board constructive criticism as well as praise.

Outside expertise can help you develop your business and stay on track. People to consult and listen to include:

→ your partner, who wants to see you succeed;
→ suppliers, who have an incentive to see your business grow;
→ customers, who may know better than you what they want;
→ trade associations, which allow you to benchmark your performance against similar businesses;
→ competitors, who react to the threat you pose to their livelihood;
→ your bank manager, who will spot financial trends before you do;
→ your accountant.

As you can see, the list of people who might offer you business advice is almost endless. However, there is a real danger in asking too many people for advice, in that you will find yourself confused as you try to make sense of it all. Never lose sight of the fact that it is your business, your money and your livelihood at stake.

Top Tip

Seek and welcome business advice, but follow it only if your instinct tells you it is right.

Lifestyle	High growth
Here, a mentor with knowledge of your business sector can be invaluable. Not only will they help you over the hurdles but they may also have some useful contacts.	Mentors here are more usually formally involved as non-executive directors. Usually paid, they sign up to accept legal responsibility for the company's activities.

Peer support

One of the strengths of the many business and networking groups you might consider joining is their ability to give you impartial advice. The advice you receive over a networking breakfast, for example, will not be delivered by an expert but by someone who has probably encountered the very challenge you are currently wrestling with. The academics call this peer support.

Every small business owner has an incentive to encourage and support others in the same situation. As your new business grows, you will find a tremendous camaraderie among your fellow entrepreneurs. This is not totally altruistic. A significant proportion of the new business won by the typical small enterprise is introduced or referred. In other words, you will recommend the businesses that you know and they will recommend you.

Case study
Craig Bunday, Reliant Packaging,
www.reliantpackaging.co.uk

When Craig Bunday set up a packaging and design consultancy in 2001 he knew that word-of-mouth marketing and networking were the ways to build it. He joined his local Business Club and quickly found it could deliver much more than sales leads.

As he explained to me, 'I was able to treat my weekly networking group as my management meeting: my networking referral group became my sales team, my support and, in many cases, my friends.'

▶

Although he has now moved on from this franchise, Craig is still a great advocate and believer in the concept of using word-of-mouth marketing to grow a business.

Finding a networking group to join

The Business Club is just one example of the many networking groups you can join. Many franchises are creating in themselves business opportunities for those that buy them. All provide opportunities to discuss business problems and challenges as well as seek out referrals to build your business. The Business Club is just one of many business networking organisations you can join. All provide opportunities to meet new people and become more confident at pitching your business. Most will let you attend a few meetings before joining. Try a few and join the one that suits you best.

The networks you join will depend largely on the type of business you are in. For example, if you are in a small community and your customers are local, then a local breakfast and networking group is probably right for you. If, however, you are a specialist supplier with customers spread across Europe, you might do better to join a national trade organisation.

To find the right groups for you, look at the following sources.

→ **Locally** To find your local breakfast networking club or chamber of trade and commerce look online, ask around or talk to the local government economic development team, which should be able to guide you (see BNI at **www.bni.eu/uk** and 4N **www.4networking.biz**).

→ **Regionally** For specialist sector groups, often created by local government to build the capacity and skills of a business sector that is important to the region's economy. Also look for privately run networks that meet the needs of ambitious businesses like yours.

→ **Nationally** Most types of business have a trade association that you can join. These provide specialist support, training and knowledge specific to the type of business you are running.

→ **Universities** These often run programmes for growing businesses. They may be set up as 'action learning sets', where a group of like-minded entrepreneurs share and discuss their challenges with an expert facilitator.

Sharing resources

There is much more than just tips and hints that you can share with other entrepreneurs. The value of their advice is that they are facing similar challenges to you – and finding ways round them. Sometimes the solutions and shortcuts they have developed can be of immense value to you, too.

For example:

→ you can share standard documents, such as terms and conditions of trade, employment contracts and confidentiality agreements;

→ if a sales letter is particularly effective for one company, it can be quickly adapted to work for another;

→ spreadsheets and other software calculators and shortcuts can be shared easily, making everybody more efficient.

Top Tip

Twitter and LinkedIn are both great online communities where you can ask other entrepreneurs for help. Be sure to also offer help to people asking questions for which you have the answer.

Case study
David Toohey, The Accountants Circle,
www.accountantscircle.co.uk

David Toohey launched The Accountants Circle in 2007. He had been doing contract work for a number of accountants, using their spreadsheet templates. He found these often clumsy and error-prone.

With his team, David developed a suite of more robust accountancy spreadsheets and online tools, which are made available to his members. There are now over 1,000 accountants and bookkeepers who have joined The Accountants Circle.

▶

The strength of David's company is that it enables accountants to share information and ideas with each other. It also develops and provides members with the tools and templates they need without each of them having to reinvent the wheel all the time. Peer mentoring and support of this kind is always valuable and in this case forms a profitable business.

What is a mentor and how are they different from advisers?

Most truly successful people have used a mentor to guide them along the way. Whereas an adviser may be used to dealing with a specific issue or problem, a mentor takes a more holistic view of you and your enterprise. The relationship you develop with a mentor is usually more open, more frank and longer lasting than a relationship with someone simply giving advice.

A good mentor will encourage you to set goals, reflect on decisions and be objective as you grow your business. In many ways they will share the business journey with you, without taking control, so that you have the benefit of their experience and wisdom to support you.

How to find a mentor

Before you look for a mentor, you need to know the kind of person you are seeking. Usually mentors are:

→ older than you and so in no way competitive with you;

→ more experienced in business than you;

→ better connected, with useful contacts they can introduce you to;

→ people who have failed as well as succeeded (failure can teach much more than success!)

Places to look for a mentor include:

→ The Prince's Trust – which can match you with a volunteer mentor if you are aged under 30 and seek the Trust's help before you start your business;

→ business support agencies – which often also matchmake between businesses and volunteer mentors;

→ your local business community – where there may be someone willing to share their experience and take a genuine interest in your success;

→ your industry sector – where one of the elder statesmen and women may feel that mentoring you is a good way to stay in touch with the industry in which they have spent their career.

> **Top Tip**
>
> The UK government endorses and recommends the peer mentoring website. It might be a good place for you to start your search for an effective business mentor (see **www.mentorsme.co.uk**).

The mentoring relationship

The relationship you have with your mentor can be quite informal, almost social. A mentor can be someone who takes an interest in your personal and business growth. They may be motivated to do this because they enjoy helping others and wish to share some of the knowledge and experience they have gained over the years. It can be very rewarding to steer someone away from the pitfalls into which they themselves have painfully plunged.

If you are running a limited company, it may make sense to appoint your mentor to your Board as a non-executive director. This means that they are accepting some legal responsibility for the well-being and performance of the company. You will need to pay them an annual fee, but if you choose the right person this will cost a lot less than you might think.

What is important in a good mentoring relationship is that you and your mentor:

→ meet regularly;

→ discuss all aspects of your personal and business performance;

→ do not avoid constructive criticism;

→ deal with problems as they arise;

→ do not agree with each other just to be polite.

Top Tip

Always look for a mentor who is a lot further up the entrepreneurial ladder than you. Do not limit yourself by adopting as a mentor someone only a little further ahead. A little of a high-flyer's time will be more valuable than a lot from an 'also ran'.

Frequently asked questions

The following are some typical questions that new entrepreneurs have about finding and working with a mentor or adviser.

How important are formal qualifications when choosing a business adviser?

There are specific business adviser standards and qualifications against which budding advisers may be measured. However, the most important qualification needed to give effective business help is for the adviser to have witnessed or experienced the challenges for which you are seeking their input. Also, it must be someone you can trust and whose opinion you will respect.

I've heard mixed reports about Business Link advisers. Should I seek advice from a private consultant rather than a government-funded adviser who may not be so good?

There are literally thousands of Business Link advisers and some will undoubtedly be better than others. Remember that sometimes people do not like what they hear from a business adviser because it is a little too close to the truth! Like bank managers, business advisers often get the blame for their clients' shortcomings.

▶

The market leader in my industry has just sold his company and retired. I'd like to invite him to mentor me but I'm not sure how to go about it.

First, you have to put yourself in their shoes. Will working with you give them the chance to review some of their past successes without the day-to-day grind from which retirement has just released them? Put together a list of benefits to them in helping you and then engineer an opportunity to meet them to discuss it.

Key points

→ Be wary of advice from self-appointed experts. The best advisers are those recommended to you by people you trust.

→ Business networks and relevant user groups can be good sources of free, experience-based advice.

→ Everyone will do better with the support of a good mentor.

Next step

If this chapter has left you sitting on the fence, you're probably better off getting started than hesitating. Minimise the risk by all means, but opening for business will build your confidence far more than holding back.

_____

_____

_____

_____

Timing is everything – how to decide when to start

Chapter Eleven

Deciding on the best time to start your business is a challenge in itself. If you spend too much time preparing and perhaps pondering, you will miss opportunities. If you start too soon, you may not be prepared to deal with everything that comes your way. Striking a happy balance is what this chapter will help you to achieve.

> ## Very few things happen at the right time and the rest do not happen at all. HERODOTUS

Why you might want to start up straight away

It is natural to want to have everything ready before you open the door for business. After all, if you fail to impress your first customers word will soon spread.

On the other hand, you need your customers to help you develop the right package of products or services that meet their needs. There is a danger that you will spend ages trying to guess or research what your customers expect of you when, actually, all you have to do is ask them.

Case study
Ann Macaulay, Bells Play Group,
http://bellsholidayclub.com

When Ann was made redundant from Thomas Cook in 2008 she decided it was time to be her own boss. She sought advice from Business Link and looked at her options. A parent, she wanted to work with children and knew how difficult it could be to get good childcare. After considering buying an existing business or franchise, Ann decided to start up her own playgroup.

Now her venture is well established, with playgroups running in Peterborough, and South-East London and full day nurseries in Lincolnshire and Cambridgeshire. Ann says that redundancy gave her the push she needed to work for herself. She has plans to grow her business and, as well as childcare-related training, has recently completed an MBA.

When Sir Clive Sinclair invented the C5 electric tricycle in 1985 he probably did not do enough consumer research first. To him, the idea of scooting down the road in a battery-powered plastic tube was a good one. To the motoring public and, in particular, the press, it was not.

The British Safety Council criticised the C5 on the day it was launched, commenting, 'The vehicle is too close to the ground and the driver has poor visibility in traffic.' This gave the press the negative headlines they needed and the C5 was soon history.

Had Sir Clive involved the media and various road safety experts earlier, he could have developed the product in a way they could support. It might have been quite different, but it would have stood a far better chance of market success.

Start step by step

The key to starting up straight away is to do it step by step. In other words, don't wait until you are ready for a major launch, but instead start your business a little bit at a time. Crucially, this means that your customers, suppliers and others with influence over your success can be involved early on.

The more you involve other people in the development of your business, the more likely you are to get it right. It is also far less stressful to start your business gradually than it is to start with a bang.

Here are some things you might consider.

→ Work with a potential customer or two to develop and then trial your product or service. This means you have a customer from the very beginning. Those customers will probably cover your costs and hopefully also give you a small profit. More importantly, you can use them to show others that what you are launching is tried and tested.

→ Start your business before you leave your job. Building your company gradually means that you can do this before you resign. A surprising number of people negotiate with their boss a tapered departure from employment. This means they have guaranteed income while they develop the business and their boss has plenty of time to find and train their replacement. Everybody wins.

→ Open for business with a short list of products and services and then add new ones as the opportunity (and demand) arises. It is fair to say that many people put together an extensive portfolio of products because they want to have something for everyone. Once trading, however, you soon find that 80 per cent of your customers buy 20 per cent of what you do. In other words, if you start with what you know will be most popular, you may never need to do anything else. Apple, for example, has a smaller range of phones than most of its rivals. Despite this, its phones are arguably the most sought after!

Top Tip

As a general rule, the wider the choice you give your customers, the harder they will find it to make a decision. Reducing the range can increase your sales.

Why you might choose to be more cautious

Sometimes there is no alternative to waiting and launching your business with an element of surprise. This is often the case when you

How to Start Your Own Business for Entrepreneurs

are leaving employment and planning to compete in some way with the company you are departing from (if you do this it is vital that you have taken legal advice as to whether or not your contract of employment might restrict you in this respect).

You might also choose to delay starting your business because you are worried about falling demand, perhaps caused by an economic downturn. If this is the case, work out how much market share you need to take to be successful and ensure you can be both competitive and profitable.

In times of economic crisis or market shrinkage it is the big players that have the hardest time. You, however, do not have the massive overheads and have not had years of good times to make you complacent. Furthermore, when times are tough, people are more likely to shop around. It is easier to launch yourself as a new supplier and be taken seriously in a downturn than in a boom. Unprofitable business for a big company can be very lucrative for a small one like yours.

Here are some other possible reasons for caution.

→ You have to wait for a contract period to expire. Perhaps you are taking over from another distributor or you need to wait until the terms of your former employment contract can be met.

→ Your business is seasonal and you want to coincide the launch with the peak selling period. It could make more sense, for example, to launch a home improvement business in the spring rather than midwinter.

→ There are changes in the wider world – for example, imminent legislation – that mean you are best advised to wait until a certain date, after which it will be easier for you than it is right now.

Top Tip

In general it is always better to be trading than waiting. If you do decide to hesitate, make sure the reason is a good one. Sometimes people just make excuses to themselves for putting off until tomorrow what deep down they know they should be doing today.

When do other people start a business and why?

The best time to start a business is when the opportunity presents itself. However, the opportunity may not always be obvious. Equally, convention and the people around you may try to discourage you from what they consider to be the wrong thing to do.

Here are some examples of when people started businesses that might surprise you.

Charles Dunstone was just 25 years old with £6,000 to his name when he set up The Carphone Warehouse. He saw that the market for mobile phones was growing and seized his opportunity (**www.carphonewarehouse.com**).

Anita Patel was rejected by several banks. 'They thought my idea wasn't viable and that I was too much of a risk – our family didn't own the corner shop so therefore I wasn't suited to running a business', she says. With a grant and loan from the Prince's Trust she proved the bank wrong. Today she owns the market-leading company in the field of Asian wedding planning, event management, PR and ethnic marketing (**www.tania-tapel.com**).

Anne Davidson saw a need for a magazine in rural Cheshire where she lives after being made redundant from her job in newspaper advertising at the age of 57. She took advice from PRIME (The Prince's Initiative for Mature Enterprise) and set up a very successful monthly magazine called *My Village News*.

People from all walks of life start businesses – at all ages and usually without as much money as they think they need.

How can you make the best decision for yourself?

The best time for you to start your business will probably seem obvious when you get there. Everyone's situation is different, but usually deep down you know when the time has come to push the button and start trading.

When you look back on the first few weeks and months of your business' life, you may well feel that your timing could have been

How to Start Your Own Business for Entrepreneurs

better. Unfortunately, none of us has the gift of foresight and so cannot predict what will happen in the future.

These points may seem a little philosophical for a guide to starting a business, but it is important to recognise them all the same. One of the worst things you can do is to beat yourself up because, looking back, you wish you had done things differently. Learn to look forward and not back and you'll make more progress.

Lifestyle	High growth
You may need nudging off the fence, but usually lifestyle entrepreneurs start trading when it feels right.	Not all high-growth businesses start as such. Some are lifestyle initially but 'strike gold' and go for it to capitalise on the opportunity.

Case study
John Moore, Windcrop,
www.windcrop.co.uk

John Moore was Commercial Director at Lotus Cars. He became interested in alternative energy and realised that there was an emerging market for micro-generation. Being an engineer he designed an easy-to-erect mast that could carry a 5kW turbine without needing a costly concrete base. He also calculated that if he built a fleet of turbines, he could afford to give the landowner free electricity. His own profit would come from the government's 'generation tariff', plus selling surplus power back to the National Grid.

He sought investors and launched the business at the end of 2009. Within two years he had 100 turbines installed and a further 340 contracts signed and awaiting planning consent and installation. His business has already reached critical mass, with enough turbines erected to enable him to remain profitable as government incentive payments reduce.

While not everything, timing did play a key role in Windcrop's success. John launched the company at a time when interest was growing and there were few suppliers with his level of professionalism and commitment.

Frequently asked questions

Choosing the best time to start a business can be difficult. Here are some typical questions.

I have been offered the chance of a lifetime, to be the first distributor in the UK for an innovative new health product. I had intended to stay at work until my children left school, but this really does seem too good a chance to miss. What do you think?

Rather like the number 11 bus, chances of a lifetime can be surprisingly frequent or frustratingly absent. I would advise caution in any deal where you are being pressed to make a decision quickly without having time to really research the opportunity. I am sure that even if you miss this one there will be another along later.

My employer is consolidating the business and has really lost enthusiasm for the department I run and the work that we do. Should I try to buy out the activity I manage or should I resign and start afresh?

So much depends on where you are with your personal life and circumstances. If starting a business now is what you want to do and you have the support of your family, it would make sense to open negotiations with your boss. You have nothing to lose by being open about your ambition if the work that you do is no longer considered significant to the future of your employer. Do not let yourself be pushed but, rather, choose your own time to start.

Key points

→ In general it is better to start your business as soon as you can.

→ Remember that you don't have to start your business all in one go. Do it gradually and reduce the risk.

→ You are never too old or too young to start a business.

→ Your intuition will help you decide when the time is right for you.

How to Start Your Own Business for Entrepreneurs

Next step

Look long and hard at the business you are creating. If you're too broad, you'll get lost in the marketplace. If you're too niche your market might not be large enough. Work out what 'just right' looks like for you!

_____

_____

_____

_____

Finding customers

Part Three

Where to look for the best customers

Customers are the food your business needs to nourish itself. In the same way you need food, your enterprise cannot do without customers and if you don't have enough, you soon feel hungry. Also, like food, some customers will fill you up but not really provide any lasting benefit, whereas others will be full of concentrated goodness.

Your challenge is to feed your business with a balanced diet of customers and not live hand to mouth.

> **Emergencies have always been necessary to progress. It was darkness which produced the lamp. It was fog that produced the compass. It was hunger that drove us to explore.** VICTOR HUGO

What are your marketplace boundaries?

When you start your own business, your marketplace can seem to have no boundaries. Perhaps in your employed life you became used to working in a clearly defined geographic territory or in a predetermined market sector. Now there is no one to tell you where you cannot go. The choice can be bewildering.

You need to strike a happy balance between focusing on the most obvious and easy-to-win customers and acquiring the harder-to-reach but potentially more lucrative business, too. Here's how to define your marketplace boundaries.

Starting point

The chances are high that you already know your first customers. You may not recognise them as such, but they are there all the same. This is because most people start a business in a place or industry where they already have contacts and some experience. Your first customers could be:

→ previous employers who know you and have confidence in what you do;

→ people you have been doing business with on behalf of your employer who will be keen to support your new venture;

→ family and friends within your social circle who know about your business plan and have encouraged you thus far.

It is not unusual for a new entrepreneur to feel that recruiting their former boss as their first customer is somehow cheating. They wrongly believe that to do business properly you have to sell to people you do not know. As a rule, your first customers should be the people you can sell to most easily. If you're worried about breaking the terms of an employment contract, take legal advice. Contracts often sound worse than they really are.

Geography

The most obvious marketplace boundary is defined by geography. If you run a corner shop, your customers will all live nearby or regularly pass by your door on their way to and from work. If you are an accountant, your clients will mostly live and work within your wider community or have some link with it. Although there is no logical reason why an accountant should not have clients spread all over the country, most are recognised and benefit from building a client base close to home, if only for convenience.

Once you start to specialise, geography becomes less important. For example, if your passion was model railways, you might drive 50 miles to visit a specialist shop. Equally, if you were an accountant specialising in showbiz celebrities, your clients might well be spread all over the world.

When you are looking at the geographical area from which you will recruit your customers, consider the following.

→ How big an area you will have to cover to find enough of the right kinds of customers. There is no point in going too far, but not going far enough limits your potential.

→ Which competitors are active within that area and how you are going to win customers from them?

→ Any relevant market trends or changes. For example, if you are a shopkeeper in an area where slums are being replaced by trendy apartments, you might need to revamp your shop and stock higher-quality products.

Face to face or virtual

If you shop at your local bookshop, you will only travel to the closest branch. If you shop on Amazon, the physical location of the retailer is of no interest to you. The transaction is conducted online and the goods delivered to your door. The decision to trade online or face to face is a difficult one. Many companies choose to do both, often starting online and then opening retail outlets as their customer base grows.

As a rule of thumb, you can sell commodities online more easily than added-value products that need interpretation, personalisation or to be handled before you buy. For example, you would probably buy an MP3 player from a website, but visit a shop to buy a guitar.

Case study
Ian Clarke, Pansophix,
www.pansophix.co.uk

Ian Clarke developed a passion for organisational consultancy while working for BT. With former colleague Steve Westall he launched a training company in 2004. They started off providing both face-to-face and online soft skills training to corporate clients.

Most of their clients are large organisations in the public, private and academic sectors. From a big company background themselves, Ian and Steve understand the issues and challenges their clients are facing. They are confident, too, that the face-to-face training they provide meets the customers' needs and are able to back this up via impressive feedback questionnaire results and client testimonials.

The marketplace has, however, been changing, with increasingly accessible content now expected and demanded on mobile devices like the iPod and the iPad.

Responding to this change they have developed an impressive range of downloadable eBooks (42 'Useful Guides' and growing) and provide 'Useful Guide Libraries' to organisations that want to offer these as part of their training solution. Clients select the soft skills topics they need for their 'Useful Guide Library', which provides unlimited access to all staff 365 days per year as part of a cost-effective annual subscription.

Responsiveness is still the key to success and many of their 'Useful Guide' titles have been driven by demand from clients, who continue to renew their subscriptions as the portfolio expands and their people benefit from the training.

How to Start Your Own Business for Entrepreneurs

Why you need to look beyond the obvious

To start with, you need to look for the obvious customers. There really is no point in making life difficult. However, it is worth spending a little time looking beyond the obvious. That is where you find the new market opportunities or the customer group you had not previously considered. For example:

→ a hotel situated one hour from an airport can market itself to inbound travellers arriving from other countries;

→ a contract gardening company working for affluent householders might also offer a service to estate agents needing empty or neglected properties tidied up;

→ a tourist attraction might offer itself as a corporate hospitality venue during the winter when it would otherwise be closed.

Established businesses often discover these new opportunities by chance. An unusual order or approach from someone unlike your typical customer can alert you to the fact that people have found new ways to use what you sell. If you receive an unusual request from a prospective customer, take the trouble to find out what it is they had in mind. Then you can perhaps make them the first of many.

Not all of these will be things you want to encourage. For example, young people who sniff glue will not be welcome customers in any DIY store!

Lifestyle	High growth
It's easy to focus on what you like and miss what your customers might prefer. Don't miss obvious opportunities to sell new things to your customers.	To grow fast, you need to really know your customers and meet their changing needs. The better you know your customers, the better you will know how to satisfy their needs and grow your business.

Why you need to keep looking when you're busy

If you are going to be working on your own, as most new entrepreneurs do, you will inevitably find yourself incredibly busy at times. It can be difficult to continue searching for new customers when you are overwhelmed with business.

The fact is that the period you are busy is when you have to look harder for new business. This is because new customers often take time to recruit and you want to avoid having a large gap between completing your current projects and starting the next batch.

When you talk to established businesspeople they will sometimes talk about 'feast or famine'. This is a cycle that they fall into, where they are busy selling, then busy delivering what they have sold, then lacking in new customers for a while until they have recruited new ones.

The most successful entrepreneurs are those that continue to sell all the time. Always allocate some time for finding new customers, however busy you are.

Top Tip

You're never too busy to look for new business. In fact, the best time to look for new business is when you're busy. People like doing business with busy people! Set aside some time every week to market your business.

How can you do this easily without spending too much?

There are plenty of market research companies and other consultancies eager to sell you their services. As your business grows, you may well find it worthwhile engaging experts to help you identify and reach out to new markets. For now, though, it makes sense to do things yourself. The following are some simple techniques you might try.

→ Look for published customer lists on competitors' websites. These can give you an insight into the kinds of customers you could aim for.

→ Visit shopping centres if you are in retail to see what kinds of people shop in outlets like yours. Don't be afraid to stop and question the occasional person and to be honest about why you are conducting research.

→ Search for your own products or services on the internet. You might be surprised by what you find.

→ Survey your first customers to find out how they found your business and what they like or dislike about what you do. If encouraged, they can suggest places and people you might consider in your quest for new customers.

→ Once you are trading and marketing your business, use offer codes or simply ask your customers how they heard about you. You can then look for more people from the same sources.

Case study

Michael Eccles, Hideaways in Hay,
www.hideawaysinhay.co.uk

Michael is an entrepreneur and former city management consultant. With his wife Séza he has created a unique short break holiday destination at his home on the Welsh/English border.

Although Hay is a popular destination for booklovers, Michael recognised that, to maintain high occupancy levels all year round, he needed to proactively market his business. His website carries a testimonial from discerning restaurant critic Giles Coren and, on many pages, Michael's voice appears to help you find your way round. He also encourages visitors to leave reviews on Trip Advisor, as he knows this can drive traffic to his website.

But what earns Michael a mention in this book is the way he has built a large database of prospective customers. He runs competitions with free peak weekend breaks as prizes. I am on that list and, although I've yet to visit, I feel I already know Michael and recognise the high standard of accommodation he provides.

Frequently asked questions

Here are some of the questions new entrepreneurs ask about finding customers.

My business will supply and fit carpets in people's homes. Everyone is therefore a potential customer. How can I define my market and where should I start?

It makes sense to concentrate on one particular type of home or person. Perhaps you could concentrate on your immediate neighbourhood so that your customers are close together and will soon see you as the local carpet fitter. In other words, grow a reputation quickly by working locally.

I like restoring classic cars and had been asked by my uncle to take over his motor engineering business. It is in a rural village and so, apart from a few stalwart customers, finding new ones will be difficult. Any suggestions?

This is definitely an opportunity to focus on classic cars and attract customers from far and wide. I know of a village garage that has survived by focusing almost exclusively on Volkswagen Beetles. Not only does the business restore and repair old Beetles but it also has a thriving online business in parts and accessories.

I want to sell fashion accessories online. I'm pretty confident I can get the right products into my range, but how can I define and, more importantly, reach my market?

Your website will be one of thousands selling similar products to the world at large. To succeed you will have to focus. You can focus either on one particular kind of customer – for example, young mums who are too busy to go out to the shops – or on one kind of product. To offer everything to everyone will not enable you to build a relationship with your customers.

How to Start Your Own Business for Entrepreneurs

Key points

→ Your first customers need to be those who are easiest to recruit.

→ Do not pass potential customers on your way to finding new business further afield.

→ Specialising makes it easier for you to find (and be found by) new customers.

→ If you start an online business, don't rule out working face to face once you've built a customer base.

Next step

As you reflect on brand, remember that although you can see the flaws, others will only see what you show them. Branding is about being bold.

_____

_____

_____

_____

How to develop the right brand and image

Chapter Thirteen

Your appearance, experience, attitudes and behaviour define your personality. It is these characteristics and the perceptions they create that people use to judge you. Do they want to be your friend or would they prefer you went away? Your new enterprise will also develop a personality and it is equally significant. The personality of a business is called its brand.

What is brand?

To most people, brands are synonymous with the products they represent. That is because most brand awareness is created by people who are marketing consumer products. The marketer develops logos, jingles and advertising campaigns that build and reinforce the aspects of their products that they want you to appreciate and value.

A well-managed brand will use marketing techniques and campaigns to focus the consumer on recognising its key points of difference. For example, Volvo cars have always positioned themselves as being very safe. BMWs, however, are seen as something to aspire to that, surprisingly, is just within reach. Hyundai focuses on the fact that its cars are usually cheaper (but equally reliable) than those of the better-known brands.

When you start a business, you probably do not have the budget to artificially create the customer perceptions and beliefs you wish to encourage. That does not mean developing and managing your brand is not important. It means you have to do things differently.

If you are the entrepreneur launching a new company, it will almost inevitably mirror many of your personal traits and values. That is because you have had the original idea, developed the plan and created the organisation. As your business grows, it literally takes on a life of its own, giving yours back to you. Managing the transition can be difficult, but that is where your business begins to acquire real value as it is no longer perceived to depend on you for its success.

 In great affairs men show themselves as they wish to be seen; in small things they show themselves as they are. NICHOLAS CHAMFORT

Case study

John Hope, Hope Technical Developments,
www.hope-tecdev.com

John Hope runs a long-established, family-owned company in Berkshire. It designs and markets a range of aftermarket products for commercial vehicles. All are connected with operator and vehicle safety.

It is best known for the 'Safe T' bars. These are strong steel bars that are mounted on the backs of vans and lorries to protect the vehicles from damage. They also help absorb the impact in the event of a rear end shunt.

Each bar has a red reflective strip that has 'Safe T bar' printed on it. Not only does this promote Hope's brand to everyone who sees the product, it also enables customers to show that they care about safety, too. It's a great example of effective branding.

Why you need to get your brand and image spot on

However small your new business, you want it to look attractive to prospective customers. You also want the customers you recruit to talk positively about your products or services to people they know. Word of mouth is the most powerful way in which news of your enterprise will spread. Having a strong brand and clear image will help achieve that.

The following are some key elements of branding that will take you in the right direction.

Focus

The more specific your customer proposition, the easier it will be for people to recognise it. For example, imagine you are a motor engineer with a garage in a small town. You repair and maintain cars. If you promote yourself as being able to do anything to any make of any age, you will attract some customers. Probably most will be people looking for someone conveniently close by.

However, if you want to attract customers from further afield, you will need to specialise. Furthermore, as a specialist, your business name and the whole customer experience will need to be tailored to fit your specialism.

If your expertise and inclination encouraged you to specialise in high-performance sports cars, you might set up your business to look like a racing track pit stop – somewhere people go to have highly complicated tasks completed quickly and efficiently.

If, however, you decide to focus on women drivers, you would create a much softer and non-threatening environment. You would set out to demonstrate how you can be trusted. You would also add such services as free collection and return. That way, female drivers can choose to avoid visiting what they might see as a macho workshop environment.

As you can see, the same business focused on a different market sector might have a completely different look, name and package of services and serve a completely different customer group.

Name

The name you give your business should make it very clear what your business does. Ideally it should convey some benefit message as well. If, for example, a florist's shop is named after its owner, say 'Smith's', you would have to see the shop to know what it does. A better option would be to call it something like 'Beautiful Blooms' or even 'Flower Arrangers' Heaven', if it sells flowers and the accessories used by people keen on flower arranging.

Case study
Martin Price, Sinsins Lovestore,
https://twitter.com/#!/sinsinsmartin

Like so many people, Martin once visited a traditional 'adult shop' and found the experience embarrassing and tawdry. 'The products were of low quality, the customer service non-existent and the emphasis was on sleaze', he said.

Such a negative experience prompted him to open his own, friendly and far from seedy, Sinsins Lovestore in Norwich. Breaking new ground with a down-to-

▶

How to Start Your Own Business for Entrepreneurs

earth, positive, healthy and fresh approach, Martin's shop is bold, bright, light, modern and easily puts people at ease with its romantic and sensual array of goods aimed at both men and women.

Sinsins is more than just a shop; Martin also goes out into the local community giving talks to a wide range of professional bodies. He promotes a strong emphasis on information and education. As a direct result of this, many Relate counsellors, GPs and other health professionals often refer their clients to Sinsins Lovestore.

Martin chose the name of his business to be both light-hearted and explicit. 'I wanted to get across that we're about love and relationships,' he said, 'and to prove that all things sexual can be done with taste and respectability. The store name is a play on words, "without sins".'

Carl failed to connect the choice of name for his business with the lack of customers.

Carl's Gulp and Burp Cafe

Top Tip

Make it obvious from your business' name what you do and how you are different.

Appearance

Appearance in terms of brand means much more than just your logo. You will know that many major brands are recognisable from only their logo. The Nike 'swoosh' is a good example and the McDonald's 'golden arches' is another. A glimpse of either immediately creates in your mind an expectation of what will be delivered by the company behind the logo.

A new business, by definition, does not have an established brand or logo. You have to concentrate on creating good first impressions so that your customers come back time and time again. Of course, a good logo can help, but in reality it is what your customer sees that you have to get right. Consider the following examples.

→ **Colour** The paint on the walls, the fascia of your shop, the clothes you wear and the letterhead on which you send your mailshot all need to be the right colour for the field you are in. Just as a funeral director would not adopt bright red as its business colour, so a trendy interior design company should not look black and sombre.

→ **Light** Nightclubs are dimly lit to create ambience and atmosphere. Bookshops are brightly lit so that people can read before they buy. Even a solicitor's office can be lit in such a way that it reassures and comforts the nervous customer, anxious to have a contract worded correctly. Think of your business as a theatre and light it appropriately for what will take place there.

→ **Sound** The right background music can set the scene of the transactions you wish to conduct. It has been proven in retail outlets that the right background music will encourage people to stay longer and spend more. Equally, banging, crashing and swearing from a workshop adjacent to the room in which you meet customers will not encourage them to buy what is being manufactured next door. Think about what your customers hear.

→ **Smell** Just as the aroma of freshly brewed coffee and recently baked bread will help you to sell your house or flat, so, too, will your business benefit from smelling sweet. If nothing else, always have fresh flowers and fruit on your meeting room table.

Lifestyle	High growth
Brand is important for even the most modest enterprise. It's what makes it easy for people to keep coming back for more. Be memorable.	In the fast-growing business, brands can develop identity and acquire value independently of the organisation. Achieve this and you can sell off brands without selling the company.

How to Start Your Own Business for Entrepreneurs

Buying design

Most businesses, established and new, depend on graphic design to communicate their brand messages clearly to their audience. The style in which you first alert your prospects to the opportunities you offer should be reflected in every aspect of your customers' experience. From initial mailshot to delivery of the product or service, there needs to be a consistency of image and style.

Graphic design is one of those businesses that it is very easy to start. Consequently, you will find all sorts of design companies when you start looking. This can be confusing. You have to choose between the expensive, established and highly professional design agency and the cheap and cheerful, recently started young designer who works from home. Here are some tips to help you get the best value when buying design.

1 **Know what you want** Without a clear idea of what you want your prospects and customers to know and think about you (and do as a result of becoming aware of you) your marketing will fail.

2 **Write a brief** Write a single page that details your marketing objectives. What exactly do you want the designer to produce and how will you measure the success of their work?

3 **Find three designers** Ask people you know to make recommendations or find out who produced work that has particularly impressed you.

4 **Meet them** When you meet each designer, give them the time to talk you through their work portfolio, then invite them to comment on your brief. Remember that designers are creative people and you need to give them every opportunity to create ideas for you. Most designers will produce some visuals to illustrate what they can do. They do not expect to be paid for these, appreciating that this is part of the selling process.

5 **Choose one** Your choice of designer should not be made purely on price. Stunning, innovative design that really positions your business should generate more profit and therefore be worth paying a premium to acquire.

6 Let them do their job The biggest problem designers encounter with new clients is where the client wants to be totally involved in the project. Of course, it is important that you see the work develop and, are consulted when decisions are to be made, but do not inhibit your designer by micro-managing the project. Give them enough leeway to surprise and impress you.

> ## Top Tip
>
> The clearer you make your brief, the better the designer will translate it into images and the fewer drafts will need to be done.

A sample design brief

For an example, let's say you run a health and safety consultancy. You have 20 years' experience as a government inspector. You know that very few businesses will willingly volunteer to invest in health and safety advice; most think that they can sort it out for themselves and hiring a consultant will somehow lead to them spending a lot of money on upgrading their facilities.

By paying you instead to look at a business and telling them what they don't need to do as well as perhaps what they do need to do, you will set yourself apart from your competition. Based on this, you want to be seen as:

→ a 'recycled' inspector who knows how inspectors think;

→ independent and not interested in selling anything apart from your time;

→ determined to save your clients' money, not spend their money;

→ qualified and up to date.

You will need stationery, a website and perhaps a simple leaflet.

Winning words

As well as choosing a descriptive and memorable name for your business, there are many other ways you can use words to give your enterprise a boost. Straplines and slogans, for example, can convey the benefits you offer in a very effective way. The words you use in your promotional material need to be clear, concise and written with the reader in mind.

> **When I make a word do a lot of work, I always pay it extra.** RENÉ MAGRITTE

Here are a few techniques you might consider.

→ **Straplines** These can benefit hugely from being short and succinct, using techniques such as alliteration (where all words start with the same letter) – for example, 'Brunch at Betty's Bumper Buffet'. Similarly, 'Mr Nuisance Pest Control' is effective because pests are a nuisance.

→ **Context** If you know where your words will be read, you can tailor them to that situation. For example, you could have great fun with an advert for smoke detection on the back of a bus.

→ **You** This is one of most the powerful words in the English language. Too often new entrepreneurs write about what 'we' do rather than how 'you' will benefit. For example, 'We have the widest range of car batteries in town' versus 'Whatever you drive, you will find the new battery you need here'. The point is that the customer only wants one battery and is not interested in the other 500 you have in stock.

Frequently asked questions

The following questions show some of the concerns new entrepreneurs have about branding.

Brand is difficult for us because our business is totally unique. No one else does what we do and it is difficult to describe easily what the customer can expect. What should we do?

If your business really is so specialised and your customers have nothing to compare it with, you should consider using a metaphor. In other words, compare your business to something the customer is familiar with and will understand. For example, a specialist cleaning company that undertakes difficult tasks could describe itself as a firm of 'cleaning commandos'.

We are taking over an existing business and feel rather stuck with a name we would not have chosen ourselves. There is a customer base and we don't want to risk losing it by changing the name. Any ideas?

There are two things you can do to show that the business is now different, but has not lost the essence of what it was before. The first is to place the word 'new' in front of the name. The other is to add a strapline that clearly defines how the business is now different. Both can be quite effective.

I bought some desktop publishing software for my PC and plan to create my own logo and literature. Surely this is a sensible way to keep costs down?

If you are a talented graphic designer and objective enough to step back from your business and see it through the eyes of others, then, yes, producing your own promotional material can save you money. If, however, you are worried about the professional image you are going to project and would welcome creative ideas from others, you should hire a designer.

Key points

→ Even if you're setting up a one-person company, brand is important. It's how you encourage people to see you in the best light.

→ Choose a name for your business that makes it obvious what you do and why you're different from the competition.

→ Prepare a clear brief before hiring a graphic designer to work on your image. This will ensure that you really work out what you want.

Next step

Check what you've written and see how clearly you're describing what you do. If in doubt, simply write it as you'd say it.

_____

_____

_____

_____

Marketing in a nutshell

Chapter Fourteen

Marketing is the process by which your products and services move from concept to customer. Everything in this third section could be described as marketing, but let's pause and look at the bigger picture. You see, marketing is much more than just promotion. It is also the process by which you work out what you are going to sell and at what price.

If you sell the right things to the right people at the right price you will make a profit. If you have the wrong product or service, or sell at the wrong price, you will make a loss.

> **Authentic marketing is not the art of selling what you make but knowing what to make. It is the art of identifying and understanding customer needs and creating solutions that deliver satisfaction to the customers, profits to the producers and benefits for the stakeholders.** PHILIP KOTLER

What is marketing all about?

Your passion, past experience, present opportunity and ambition have driven your decision to start a business in a particular sector or location. You have already looked at your business plan, at how you are different from your competitors and at how you will find and communicate with your customers.

These are all things you are doing because it's what you want to do. Taking a wider look at marketing than just promotion will enable you to do what you like doing, as profitably as possible. Let's look at your marketing plan. The process will help you make sure that you have not overlooked any important opportunities. It will also enable you to check the reality and achievability of your business plan.

There are four elements to marketing, often referred to as the four Ps: products/services, promotion, place and pricing.

Products/services

You have probably already worked out what your products and services are going to be – they are the things you are going to offer that people will pay for – but have you remembered everything? It can be surprising what people will buy.

Here's an exercise that will help you to make sure you're not missing out. Create a table with what you can offer along one axis and the customer types you can most easily reach along the other. Your current or planned products and services should then be plotted on to the table. You may find gaps – and it is filling these in with products or services you might otherwise have overlooked that makes this exercise worthwhile. Let's look at how Suzie, a personal trainer, did the exercise:

	Fitness assessments	*Training programmes*	*Training supervision*	*Diet advice/ food hampers*
Busy people who want to keep fit	X	X	X	
People who want to lose weight	X	X	X	X
People recovering from illness	X	X	X	

Suzie quickly realised that, although she was quick to give diet advice and weekly food hampers to those seeking weight loss, her other clients were also potential customers for hampers. The difference was client motive. Rather than wanting a carefully calorie-controlled diet, many of her 'busy people' clients found shopping and cooking a chore. They tended to eat unhealthy fast food too often as a consequence.

Suzie started making up and selling hampers for them, too, containing healthy meals they only had to heat up. This saved them time and ensured they had a healthy, balanced diet. Suzie arranged for her partner and mother to do the shopping and food preparation for the hampers as she was too was busy working one-to-one with her clients. This meant she could grow her turnover and profit even when she didn't have time to recruit and work with more training clients.

Remember that everything has a value and you might be discarding or discounting things you could sell. For example:

→ a cabinetmaker bags up his wood shavings and sells them to a pet shop;

→ a business consultant sells downloadable preformatted spreadsheets that he uses with his clients.

> **Top Tip**
>
> It's always easier to sell new things to existing customers than to sell existing things to new customers.

Case study

Anthony Marett, Don't Travel Empty,
www.donttravelempty.co.uk

Anthony Marett runs a coach business and wondered how he could overcome the lost opportunity of his coaches returning empty from the airport once a group of people had been dropped off to catch their flight.

Research told him that this was a national problem and, while hauliers had specialist brokers who matched empty trucks with one-way cargoes, there was no such opportunity for coach operators.

▶

In 2008 he set up 'Don't Travel Empty' to plug that gap in the market. Not only does it help him keep his coaches full and therefore earning but he also charges a monthly subscription to other coach operators using his website to find either additional passengers or an empty coach to which they can subcontract a one-way job.

Three years later Anthony has more than 800 members and has started selling used coaches as well. The venture continues to diversify and grow.

Promotion

The ways in which you promote your products or services to your prospective customers may include using advertising, direct mail, posters, point-of-sale displays in shops, vehicle liveries and websites, among others. The way you configure and combine these different activities is commonly referred to as the marketing mix.

Your marketing mix will largely depend on the type of business you are in. Some of the detail about how to do this can be found in Chapters Twelve to Seventeen, but here the important point to make is that you should measure the effectiveness of all your promotional activity. You can do this in the following ways.

→ By finding out where your enquiries or sales came from. What was it that encouraged the buyer to come to you?

→ By reconciling the cost of promotions with the sales they generate. This means you can focus more money on the activities that deliver the best results.

→ By remembering that word of mouth is far and away the most effective form of marketing and it costs nothing.

Top Tip

It's important to keep track of your best customers and contacts. Then you can approach them at the right time, when they are changing role or direction. Signing up with **www.iko-system.com** (it's free!) can give you a daily summary of all the changes logged by your contacts in LinkedIn. Being connected with your business contacts on LinkedIn is, these days, essential.

Distribution (place)

The ways that your products or services reach the market is called your distribution. This is not as straightforward as it might first appear. You have choices to make. For example, imagine that you make decorative cat and dog collars. You can either sell them direct, through advertising, events and via your website, or through pet shops.

If you sell direct, you will have a larger profit margin but will have to invest in advertising and promotion. If you sell through retailers, they will do the promotion for you as they already have a customer base. However, they will buy from you at a significant discount on your suggested retail price.

If your vision is to be a small specialist supplier, then selling direct might be the best idea. If you plan to grow your business, employ people to make your pet collars and need a high volume of sales to keep everything moving, then working with distributors such as pet shops could be the right way forward.

The same model applies to services because you will inevitably pay an introductory commission to people who introduce you to new clients. The alternative is to spend your time and money meeting potential clients in the hope that you meet somebody at the right time.

There are many ways that you can distribute your products and services and you must consider all the alternatives carefully before making your decision. It is also quite common for companies to use more than one of these routes to market. If you do this, you can again evaluate the return on investment in each and adjust your effort and investment accordingly.

We're all working together; that's the secret.

SAM WALTON

Pricing

There are only two ways to calculate your selling price. The first is to total your costs and add a margin. The second is to charge the market value for your product or service. In an ideal world the market value of what you are selling will be a higher price than your costs plus a margin. If it is lower you have a problem.

Let's see how the pricing process works for John, who is setting himself up as a marketing consultant. He plans to sell his expertise to businesses seeking growth and introduce them to trusted associates who can provide graphic design and web development services. Before being made redundant, John had a salary of £40,000 a year.

His first attempt at calculating a day rate was to divide the number of days he felt he could work in the year (200) by the salary he was used to earning. That gave him a day rate of £200.

His second attempt resulted from his wife reminding him that as a business owner he would have overhead costs. His target income suddenly increased like this:

Salary	*£40,000*
Car	*£10,000*
Travel, etc.	*£5,000*
Home office	*£2,000*
IT	*£1,000*
Phone/broadband	*£500*
Stationery	*£1,000*
Training	*£1,000*
Subscriptions, etc.	*£500*
Total	**£61,000**

This gave him a day rate of £300.

John's third attempt involved taking a look at the market rate for marketing consultants of his calibre. He found that small start-up businesses were unlikely to pay much more than £200 a day because they could not afford more than this. Nor could they benefit from all his expertise because they were not yet big enough to grow very quickly.

He then looked at larger organisations needing more complicated, strategic input and found that they would pay £800 a day or more. He realised that if he worked for large organisations for just 100 days a year he would be better off than if he ran himself ragged working with small companies.

Remember that you're in business to make money. Look at all the options before choosing one or more routes to market. Focus on profit, not turnover.

Lifestyle	High growth
When your venture is modest, it's important to focus on your most lucrative activities. This is especially important if you work alone!	Sometimes in a growing business, it can make more sense to do lots of simple things profitably than fewer, more difficult things that command a higher price. It all depends on how easy it is to recruit people skilled in your industry.

Setting your pricing level

In the example above, John calculated how much he needed to charge per day to give himself the same income he'd enjoyed as an employee. Then he looked at the market rate for each sector and decided to target the most lucrative. This works because John is essentially selling his time.

Top Tip

If you sell your time, your income is limited by the number of hours you can work effectively in a year. If you sell ideas, expertise or products, you remove the time barrier to sales growth. Sell what you do, not how long it takes you!

You'll make more money, though, if you sell products and services rather than time. Here are some examples.

→ A consultant sells a bespoke health and safety policy that she bases on similar past projects. She charges a fixed fee so that the time her experience saves her becomes a profit to her, not a saving to her client.

→ A subcontracted engineer moves away from selling machine time 'per hour' by developing his own product and selling that instead.

Always link the price you charge to the value you add, not the costs you incur in providing the product or service. Remember that an ice-cream on the beach will always command a higher price than one in the supermarket just up the road.

When you set your price remember that:

→ only one person can be cheapest but everyone can in some way be best;

→ if you undercut others by a long way, the customer will worry about your ability to deliver;

→ it is usually more satisfying to be expensive and well prepared than cheap and rushed off your feet.

Top Tip

The more closely your selling price is linked to the value your customer derives, the more profitable you will become. Your job is to manage your costs to give you a good margin.

Case study
Zoë Rubens, sculptor,
www.zoerubens.com

The work of experienced sculptor, ceramicist and printmaker Zoë Rubens is becoming increasingly popular with art collectors in the UK and overseas. Much of her work uses discarded maps, till receipts and scrap metal. Often you can recognise the source of an object she has incorporated into a work; its provenance can add depth and metaphor to the piece.

Although her raw materials may at times cost little, if anything, Zoë's work still commands premium prices. That's because of the value she adds with her creativity, experience and dexterity in her workshop. Nobody would buy a pile of junk, but many aspire to own the things Zoë can make from junk.

Why is it so important to keep finding new customers?

Running a business is like riding a bicycle. If you stop pedalling, you'll fall over because the momentum that kept you upright has been lost.

To put it another way, a business is either growing or shrinking. There is no equilibrium, although at times it may seem so. You constantly need to recruit new customers because:

→ some will naturally go away over time;

→ you will have disputes and lose some that way;

→ as your business grows, you will outgrow many of your original customers;

→ people retire, die and go bust.

 Your most unhappy customers are your greatest source of learning. BILL GATES

Top Tip

Too often, the only person who thinks you're charging too much is you. Have confidence in your ability to add value and delight your customers.

Frequently asked questions

The following questions are typical of the kinds of concerns that new entrepreneurs have regarding marketing.

I am an engineer making specialist equipment for the livestock industry. My products are technically far superior to my cheaper rivals', but I am finding it impossible to persuade farmers to pay a premium price for my products. What should I do?

Unfortunately, technical superiority alone will not command a market premium. It is what the additional features deliver in terms of value to the customer that dictates the price they will pay. Doing a better job does not make a bigger profit if your customer, the livestock farmer, cannot see a return on their investment in your equipment. Consider developing a cheaper range.

I find it easy to win customers, but for some reason they tend to buy once and then go away. Very few call me to place a repeat order. Why could this be?

Perhaps it is because you are not asking them to place a repeat order. When you take their initial order, you must know when they will run out and need to replenish their stock. Ring them a week or two before you think they need to order, to ask them how they're getting on and to offer to send the next consignment. The fifth P word not mentioned before is 'proactive'!

We are going to make specialist polishes used by owners of antique furniture. We want to sell through antique dealers and furniture stockists, but each will carry so little stock it is expensive even to think about visiting them all. How can we get around this?

The furniture trade, in common with many others, makes extensive use of freelance sales agents. These independent salespeople work on behalf of a range of suppliers, earning commission on the orders they generate from retailers. You need to find a sales agent whose product range would be enhanced by your range of products.

Selling is another key skill for new entrepreneurs. In the next chapter you'll discover how to make the process easier, even if you find it intimidating.

Key points

→ Marketing is much more than just promotion.

→ Map your market opportunity to identify otherwise overlooked opportunities.

→ Make sure when costing your product or service that you include all costs, especially your own time.

→ Business Link can be a good place to find someone to advise you on getting this right. Sometimes you can qualify for a grant towards the cost.

Next step

Take a second look at your website. Remember that, for most people, the internet is a huge distraction as well as a huge benefit. Make sure your website is fun as well as factual.

_____

_____

_____

_____

Your winning marketing message

Chapter Fifteen

Now let's get more specific about making marketing work for you. Your marketing messages are the words you use to communicate with your target audience. These messages have to be simple to understand and make it clear that doing business with you is beneficial. They also have to be reflected in what your customer sees and experiences.

Unless you are in retail, your marketing messages will usually arrive in front of your prospective customers without you being there to explain what they mean. This is why the messages need to be clear and consistent. Your message has to be powerful and persuasive enough to encourage your prospective customer to seek more information.

Marketing messages are what you say and write about your business proposition. They are also words and phrases others will remember and pass on when speaking about your business. Memorable marketing messages can help build the reputation of your business. The cynic might describe this as propaganda, but there is nothing wrong with propaganda, providing it is telling the truth.

 The market can stay irrational longer than you can stay solvent. JOHN MAYNARD KEYNES

What makes a good marketing message?

Imagine walking into a hardware shop and asking to buy fork handles. The man behind the counter hears you ask for four candles. You both become increasingly frustrated at your inability to communicate. This situation was very funnily portrayed by TV show *The Two Ronnies* in 1976. More than 35 years later people are still laughing and talking about the sketch, but it also carries an important lesson: a good marketing message is one that can be easily understood by the people you are trying to influence.

You must remember that people are not always rational, so you have to deliver your message to them in words they will interpret in a positive way. In other words, you have to say it like your customers say it – even if you say it differently!

A good marketing message is:

→ explicit and easily understood by everyone;

→ descriptive of the positive aspects of what you are offering;

→ memorable and therefore easy to relate to other people.

The concentrated message

Here are three classic examples of good advertising straplines. Straplines are the most concentrated form of marketing message:

'*Nothing runs like a Deere.*' – John Deere Tractors
'*Go to work on an egg.*' – UK Egg Marketing Board
'*I think therefore IBM.*' – IBM computers

Each of the three examples makes it easy to remember the product name. In their way they each also convey a product benefit.

There are other places where you need to use your marketing message. These include:

→ in the names you choose for your business and your products and services – for example, 'Ron's Reliable Taxis';

→ on the signs you place outside your building – for example, 'Welcome to the home of good taste in home furnishings';

→ on all of your brochures and other sales materials.

> **Top Tip**
>
> Even if you work in a niche industry with its own jargon, create straplines that can be understood by anyone.

What are the best words to use?

To the reader, the most compelling words in the English language are 'you' and 'yours'. Using these words extensively shows that you are thinking about the reader and not yourself. Put this book down for a moment and look at a promotional website or leaflet. More often than not the writer has written about themselves. It can be off-putting, can't it?

Which of the following two versions of a marketing message do you think is more effective?

'We pride ourselves on our ability to make really tasty cakes that we know everyone will enjoy.'
'You will really enjoy our tasty cakes, baked with pride for your satisfaction.'

There is also a lot to be said for using everyday language when describing your business and its activities. You may feel that you do not have a wide enough vocabulary to do your business justice, but people too often find themselves using large and obscure words to describe a simple business proposition. Put yourself into your customers' shoes and use the words you think they will most easily understand.

 Any word you have to hunt for in a thesaurus is the wrong word. There are no exceptions to this rule. STEPHEN KING

Marketing messages are more than just words

Your marketing message is the way you communicate your brand and its values to your audience. Words are just one aspect of this.

To be effective, every aspect of your business has to reflect those words you have chosen. So, if you claim to be reliable, your business has to emphasise that reliability in everything it does. You may even need to exaggerate your promise to make sure the message sticks. For example, if punctuality is important, then a 'money back if more than five minutes late' promise will greatly reinforce that message.

Case study

Steve Challis and Julian Patterson, Konectbus,
www.konectbus.co.uk

Steve and Julian were both managers working for a large national bus operator when they decided to go it alone in 1999. They chose a name for their business that very clearly said what their buses did. They also ran direct 'fast' services as well as others that stopped at every village along a route. Lastly, they paid real attention to detail. Drivers were smartly dressed and highly motivated. Buses were modern, well-maintained and always clean.

Over the years their business grew, winning a number of park and ride contracts as well as opening up new routes. In 2010 they were approached by national operator Go Ahead Group, which acquired the business. The new owners have invested further in the organisation, building on the strong brand values upon which the founders built their business.

Steve and Julian chose to remain with the company after the sale, continuing to run it as a local operation within a national company.

Why it is important to say it simply, clearly and consistently

Have you ever played Chinese Whispers? You whisper a message to the person next to you and they pass it on to the next person along. Finally the message comes back to the person who started it. The message is spoken aloud and everybody laughs at how much it has changed.

An apocryphal example from the First World War of a message changing as it was sent down the line is 'Send reinforcements, we're going to advance', which became 'Send three and fourpence, we're going to a dance'.

You need to minimise the risk of your marketing message becoming distorted as it is transmitted from one person to the next. Worse is the fact that if it is easy to intentionally misinterpret your strapline or slogan to create something amusing or rude, people will do this!

Lifestyle	High growth
The simpler the message the more cost-effective your marketing investment will be. If your business is just you, then you'll need a few stock phrases you can use frequently to explain what you do.	Simplicity makes scaling up easier. In a fast-growing enterprise, the more your products and processes can remain the same, the less complicated you will find growth.

How to work out what to say

Your marketing messages will be most successful if they tell people what they want to hear. The things that people want to hear are the benefits that your products or services will bring to them. In other words, 'What's in it for them?'

Professional marketers call these 'buying motives'. You buy a drink because you are thirsty or a jumper because you expect to be cold. When you go to the cinema you will choose to see the film that you think will be the most entertaining. You have to write your marketing messages in a way that appeals to one or more buying motives.

Because you make these buying decisions without having tasted the drink, worn the jumper or seen the film, you are basing your judgement on the information that is available to you. That information has been provided by the people marketing those things. The more appealing you can make your product or service appear, the more likely people are to buy it.

A good way to understand buying motives is to remember this mnemonic: SPACED. It summarises the six main reasons why anybody buys anything. Here is what the letters that make up the word stand for.

1 **Security** How safe does it make you feel? Locks protect you from intruders; braces stop your trousers falling down; the breakfast cereal you ate as a child seems a safer option than one you have never tried before.

2 **Performance** How well does it do the job? A sports car is faster than a saloon; a larger computer processor will make software run more efficiently; fillet steak is more tender than sirloin.

3 **Appearance** How good does it look or how good does it make you look? Does the product carry the right designer logo? Does my bum look big in this? Do I like the colour? Has everyone else already got one of these?

4 **Convenience** How easy is the product to acquire and use? The chewing gum is in a rack next to the till; you can buy refills anywhere; 'We come to you to save you a trip into town'; 'Click here to download and pay online'.

5 **Economy** How far will it go and what value for money does it represent? Some products are marketed as being 'faster working' or 'longer-lasting'; different cars can get different miles to the gallon; 'affordable, easy-to-replace, hard-wearing parts'.

6 **Durability** How long will it last and will it still be here to support you in the future? 'Tungsten tipped for longer life'; 'bonded for your financial protection'; lifetime guarantees; 'underwritten by Lloyd's'.

Appealing to multiple motives

Running shoes are a good example of a product that appeals to all of the above buying motives. They are surprisingly complex – a fact you only appreciate if you're a serious athlete. Here's how SPACED applies to them.

→ Security – cushioned soles to protect your feet.

→ Performance – flexible so that your feet can move freely.

→ Appearance – stylish so that people know you are a serious runner.

→ Convenience – order online and return for free if not completely satisfied.

→ Economy – with the most competitively priced high-performance shoe.

→ Durability – designed to protect your feet for at least 500 miles.

The extent to which each element appeals to the buyer will depend on their priorities. The marketer's challenge is to make the running shoes appeal to as wide a spectrum of runners as possible.

Case study

Dave Wilkinson, ThinkDave.Com,

www.thinkdave.com

Dave Wilkinson started his web business when he couldn't find a web designer that he felt comfortable hiring for his then employer. He told me that too many seemed focused on their own needs rather than his as a potential customer.

After testing the water on a part-time basis, he went full time in 2007 and hasn't looked back since. I will let him tell you why he is so successful: 'I view my relationship with clients to be a personal one. I won't sell a client something they can't benefit from. I spend a lot of time speaking to clients about their business objectives, trying to understand their businesses and making recommendations based on what is already working in the industry. As the majority of my business comes from referrals, I do my best to keep my clients very happy.'

Where and how are marketing messages used?

It is always good to have a stock of positive marketing messages that can be used consistently in every aspect of your business promotion: from advertising to brochures, from letterheads to shopfronts, from websites to product labels. The more people see and hear consistent marketing messages from your company, the more likely they are to remember and act on them.

How to Start Your Own Business for Entrepreneurs

Frequently asked questions

Here are some typical concerns new entrepreneurs might voice about marketing messages after reading this book.

Our products are used in so many different situations and we do not want to limit our customers' imagination with specific marketing messages. How can we get around this?

The answer is to make that very thing your point of difference. For example, 'The versatility of our product is limited only by your imagination' summarises your point perfectly.

I started my business to do what I want to do, in the way that I think is right, to make money to support myself and my family. Why shouldn't I be proud of that and talk about my ambitions in my marketing messages?

The fact is that your customers will be more interested in themselves than they are in you. Even if your motivation is entirely selfish, your marketing messages need to focus on what your customers will gain from doing business with you.

You use the word 'propaganda' in this chapter. Why can't I spread negative information about my competitors as a way of encouraging people to do business with me?

You need to be aware that an awful lot of people take a very dim view of businesses that are critical of their competition. Your customer wants to know that you are ethical, honest and focused on being better than your competition. You may not get this across very clearly if you insist on doing down the competition.

Key points

→ Describe your business in a way that your customers will understand and value.

→ Develop a simple, benefit-focused strapline and use it everywhere.

→ Avoid jargon and acronyms at all costs.

→ Remember that 'you' is one of the most powerful words in the English language.

Next step

It's always difficult to put a value on the return you'll get from being in the public eye, but, as you plan your promotional activity, don't overlook the opportunity for serendipity. The right people will stumble across you more frequently if you are where they can easily find you.

_____

_____

_____

_____

How to make sure your website is a winner

Chapter Sixteen

The internet plays a vital role in the way all businesses operate. People wanting to know about your business will look at your website before making contact. Email is also overtaking the telephone as the preferred means of business communication. It can be quicker than trying to catch someone on the phone, even though increasingly people reply to emails using the keypad on their phone!

If you run a small business, prospective customers will research you as well as your business. This might make you feel uncomfortable, but it will happen. It's another good reason for making sure that your enterprise is in accord with the rest of your life.

What this means is that you have the opportunity to promote your business by what you are as well as what you do. For many running a small business, life and business are inextricably intertwined. Your online marketing has to reflect this practical fact.

 Design is not just what it looks like and feels like. Design is how it works. STEVE JOBS

What can the internet do for you?

The internet can enable you to reach customers, suppliers and potential collaborators you would never otherwise recruit. A good website will enable you to attract business from anywhere in the world. It can also make it easier for your existing customers to buy from you. Tesco, for example, invested heavily in creating an online superstore where you can do your week's shopping and have it delivered to your door. Tesco's online shop saw 30 per cent sales growth in 2010.

Your website can do things that you could not possibly achieve otherwise.

→ People can find out about your business and maybe buy from you at any time of the day or night.

→ You can update your website at a moment's notice so that people can have access to the latest information, offers and opportunities straight away. They can also subscribe to an RSS (see below) feed that will update them whenever you add new content.

How to Start Your Own Business for Entrepreneurs

→ Your website can allow you to punch well above your weight. A small company with a good website can appear far more professional than a large company with a poor website.

→ Your website can collect contact details of people interested in your products or services. You can then send them regular updates by email at minimal cost.

→ You can develop a specialist business and market it effectively in ways that would just not be possible offline.

Top Tip

RSS stands for 'Really Simple Syndication'. It enables you or your customers to receive automatic updates when new content is published on a website to which you have subscribed. Google enables you to personalise your browser web page to show RSS feeds. It's a great way for people to find out what's new without having to think about it.

Case study
Roz Mita, Mannakin,
www.mannakin.co.uk

Roz admits that she has always been working on one business idea or another. She ran a successful African art company for ten years and then a web and publishing business in Malawi.

Back in the UK, she was working in retail consultancy when she spotted a gap in the mannequin market. Her company buys and sells used mannequins and parts, as well as restoring damaged dummies to pristine condition.

Half of her work comes via Google and the rest by word of mouth. Roz spends a lot of time maintaining her search engine rankings so that people searching for mannequins find her first.

Roz's website is her shop and Google her shop window.

Why some websites work and some don't

There are two kinds of website: those that are primarily for entertainment and those that are primarily for the promotion of products and services. Entertainment websites are used to build loyalty to consumer products. For example, a fizzy drinks company might create an interactive website with games, competitions and free downloads as part of a wider marketing campaign.

It is more likely that you want your website to promote your business, gather enquiries and perhaps enable people to buy from you online. In that case, your website needs to be:

→ focused very clearly on what it is you want people to know and think about your business;

→ easy to navigate and quick to download;

→ accessible by all your potential customers (a good web design company can advise you on how to achieve this);

→ interactive, so that as many people as possible will leave you their details.

Top Tip

It's really easy now to record short video clips and embed them in your website. Video enables you to talk to your prospective customer as if you were with them. The most compelling video is not always the most professional, but the most honest and sincere.

Page layout

There is little point in trying to reinvent the wheel when it comes to web page layout. You want your website to communicate quickly and effectively and to do this it needs to present the information where people expect to be able to find it.

If you look at some of the most visited news websites that have constantly changing content, you will see that they all follow the same layout. Good examples are the BBC (**www.bbc.co.uk**), the *Financial Times* (**www.ft.com**), *The Economist* (**www.economist.com**) and *The Wall Street Journal* (**http://europe.wsj.com**).

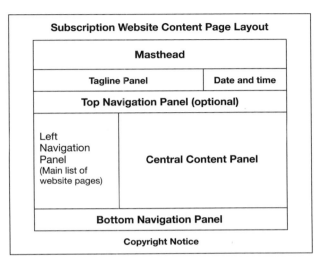

Subscription Website Content Page Layout

Masthead	
Tagline Panel	Date and time

Top Navigation Panel (optional)	
Left Navigation Panel (Main list of website pages)	Central Content Panel
Bottom Navigation Panel	
Copyright Notice	

The following are the elements of a successful web page.

→ Masthead across the top. This is where you will find the title of the page and all logos and so on that reinforce the brand.

→ Primary navigation bar down the left-hand side. This navigation bar usually appears across the whole website. It should list all the main categories of the website so that users can find their way round from any page.

→ Time and date – on any articles that you add. These show that the website is current, even if automatically updated.

→ Bottom menu bar. This tends to contain links to terms and conditions, privacy statement, site map and so on.

→ The central panel. This displays the main content of the page, including any links to other useful pages.

→ Search box at top right on every page – this enables people to search the entire website.

Make sure that your website contains a site map. This not only provides alternative navigation for visitors to your site, but is also used by search engines when indexing the site.

Top Tip

Link your Twitter feed to your website so that your most recent Tweets appear on the home page. Also add Twitter and Facebook buttons to your website so that people visiting your website can click and stay in touch. Integrate your web presence.

Content

Many people choose to create their own website and many more use content management systems to edit their own sites. This means that what you write and paste into your website can go live within minutes. There are many providers of the basic website framework into which you can add your own content. One of the best, which also provides a lot of useful articles, is **www.subhub.com**. A better known one is **http://wordpress.com**.

Before adding content to your website it is wise to do the following.

→ Run a spellcheck as it's surprisingly easy to miss typos and spelling errors.

→ Have someone else read what you have written and check that it makes sense to them.

→ Reduce the size (resolution) of pictures so that they download quickly when the page is viewed. This is really important if your website is viewed from locations with slow internet speeds.

Top Tip

Content management systems enable you to go into your website to edit and add new content. Search engine ranking improves if you regularly add new, relevant content.

How to Start Your Own Business for Entrepreneurs

How to get value for money from your website

As a rule of thumb, money invested in a website is money well spent. No organisation is credible without one and a poor website will reflect badly on your business.

It is very easy to build your own website. Unless you have an eye for design and are confident enough to build from scratch, consider hiring a developer to create the website for you. Even if they use a proprietary platform such as Wordpress, a professional developer will probably create a more exciting website. Then you can add the content and keep the site up to date.

Make sure you monitor traffic to your website. You can do this by logging in to a display of the statistics behind your website or using Google analytics.

Top Tip

Take time to look at the websites of businesses like yours before you create your own. Note what you like and what you don't. Make sure you are different!

Case study
Andy Harris, Custwin,
www.custwin.co.uk

As an employee in the dot-com boom, Andy Harris saw plenty of examples of what not to do to succeed with business websites. As he told me, 'Numerous businesses went to the wall due to flaky business models and lack of customer focus.'

Andy started writing e-newsletters packed with practical tips and soon found himself being asked to help companies with their web marketing. Eleven years on, his blogs and monthly e-newsletter consistently help people, while generating new clients for him. He is a firm believer in becoming viewed as an expert through giving away free and regular information without a heavy sales pitch.

▶

Here are his top three tips on how to gain success from a business website.

1 Closely analyse website visitors, including which companies visitors come from. Andy recommends **www.a1webstats.com**.

2 If a website isn't converting a bare minimum of 5 per cent of visitors to enquiries/ sales then pause any investment in marketing and fix the website problems.

3 Type relevant search phrases into Google to see which competitors appear. Take their website strengths and then exceed them within your own website.

Trading online

There can be few things more satisfying than logging on to your computer in the morning and finding that people have been buying from you online.

Not surprisingly, an awful lot of people have set up e-commerce websites – and many have rapidly become disillusioned and disappointed. However, providing you have the right offer and your website is easy to find, online trading can be very successful. A good place to start is eBay (**www.ebay.co.uk**). If you are not familiar with this online trading platform it is worth spending some time exploring it. The help section of the website is packed with tips and hints about online trading.

> ### Top Tip
>
> Why not set up an eBay shop to test the water to see whether e-commerce is for you? It's low cost and you benefit from the vast visitor numbers to the eBay website. Some people integrate their eBay shops into their websites and sell primarily through them.

How to sell online

As well as selling your goods or taking bookings for services, you can sell downloadable products such as software templates and podcasts. Remember that people will buy anything that saves them time and money.

If you are selling physical goods, you do not necessarily have to hold them in stock yourself. There are fulfilment specialists who will warehouse your inventory and dispatch it to your customers on your behalf as each order is received.

To enable e-commerce, you need to have a shopping cart and secure payment processing integrated into your content site. The shopping cart enables buyers to select one or more items to buy and then takes them through the checkout process.

The payment processing can be done via a 'payment service provider' such as PayPal (**www.paypal.com**).

If you are expecting to do a lot of online business it makes sense to set up your own merchant account with a bank. PayPal is cheaper to use if you have fewer transactions. Once your online business grows, it will cost you less to set up a merchant account. Remember that payment service providers make their money by taking a percentage commission on each transaction made.

There are lots of online trading platforms that you can add to your website or access from it. Research the options thoroughly before making your choice.

Lifestyle	High growth
Many businesses trade exclusively online. It's low cost and means you can work from home at times that suit for you.	Don't underestimate the investment needed to grow a robust, reliable and resilient online business that can keep growing.

Other money-making options

As well as the obvious products and services, there are other ways you can make money from your website. These include the following.

→ **Advertising** You can encourage non-competing businesses to buy banner advertising on your site. Easier to manage and less intrusive are text advertisements that contain links to the sponsor's website. You can easily add these to your website via **www.google. com/adsense**.

→ **Affiliates** You promote another business on your website and earn a commission when people click through and buy. The best-known example of this is **https://affiliate-program.amazon.co.uk/gp/associates/join**.

→ **Subscriptions** People pay a monthly fee to access specialist content on your website. You set up your site to have a members area that only subscribers can access.

> ### Top Tip
>
> If a product or service won't sell offline, it is unlikely to be a success online. Where possible, make sure people want what you're offering before marketing it online.

Spam

Some people play the numbers game by spamming – that is, sending huge numbers of emails advertising a product. This method is noted for being used by distributors of illegal pharmaceuticals and various sex aids. Many servers filter out such mass mailing. This way of conducting business does nothing for your reputation and little to build customer loyalty and, in some cases, it is illegal. In the UK, regulations enacted in 2003 state that online marketers can send email pitches and SMS messages only to consumers who have agreed beforehand to receive them, except where users are existing customers of a particular company. Don't spam!

Frequently asked questions

The following are questions that new entrepreneurs often ask about websites.

We've set up a website but it does not seem to be attracting much traffic. How can we get more people to visit our website?

There is a real science to the art of attracting traffic to a website. There are obvious things you can do, such as adding the words to your website that the search engines look for (these are known as 'keywords'). Many website templates provide boxes into which you can type the keywords that you think people would use to search for the product or service you offer. If this is confusing, it might be worth asking your web developer to introduce you to a 'Search Engine Optimisation' (SEO) specialist. These are people who make their living helping others attract visitors to their website. If you'd prefer to learn how to do it yourself, there are plenty of courses available where you can be trained by SEO experts.

A friend told me that the more generic I can make the domain name then the more likely it is that people will find my website easily. Is this true?

Personally, I would not spend a lot of money buying generic domain names. I would prefer to invest in good-quality search engine optimisation (see previous answer).

We have set up our website with a fantastic content management system. The problem is that we never seem to have time to update it with new content. Have you any tips?

What you need is a freelancer, ideally with journalism training, who can interview you regularly to find out what you need on your website and then write and post articles on your behalf. Look for someone affordable, literate and with an eye for detail.

Key points

→ Your website is your shop window to the world, so make sure it projects the best possible image of your business.

→ Remember that your time may not be best spent fiddling with your website. Do not be slow to hire professional help.

→ Experiment with e-commerce using eBay and PayPal before investing large amounts of money in a full e-commerce web solution.

Next steps

Before moving on, reflect on the people you meet and the places you go. Marketing can be no more complicated than making sure everyone you meet knows what you do.

_____

_____

_____

_____

How to get good PR and keep on getting it

Chapter Seventeen

People believe what they read in the newspapers, hear on the radio and see on TV. Becoming part of the news is what public relations (PR) is about. What's more, compared to the cost of advertising, PR can represent good value for money. Being reported positively in the press is very good for your credibility.

The good news is that you don't have to hire an expensive PR agency to do this for you. Increasingly, journalists like to hear from you direct or to find you easily when researching a news story. What counts most is the relevance and strength of your story, not the name of the person or agency submitting it.

The first thing to do if you want to publicise your business in this way is to read the publications, listen to the radio stations and watch the TV channels that your customers do. Get to know which journalists cover the kinds of topics your story might be about. Cut out and keep stories about competitors and start to see what makes a good news story.

> **There is no such thing as bad publicity except your own obituary.** BRENDAN BEHAN

What is PR really all about?

People have an innate preference for the familiar. They are reassured by familiar brands and will stay with one supplier until something goes wrong, or until you come along and persuade them to try something different.

PR is all about building awareness of your business, your products and services and yourself. It is by making people familiar with your enterprise that you will encourage them, in time, to do business with you.

Never underestimate the importance of building and maintaining your personal profile among your customer community. People buy from people – and you want people to buy from you. Many new entrepreneurs are coy about seeking personal publicity but really they should not be.

Here are a few examples of the power of publicity and PR:

→ Good press reviews will encourage more people to go to see a film.

→ Businesses will enquire about new software that they have read about in their trade press.

→ People will visit a new shop if a celebrity is cutting the ribbon.

→ A news story about how an alternative therapy has helped someone deal with a health problem will encourage other sufferers to telephone that therapist.

Case study
The atheist bus campaign,
www.humanism.org.uk/bus-campaign/

Political blogger Jon Worth used his blog to appeal for people to pledge £5 to fund a campaign of atheist ads on London buses. He felt it important to respond to a recent campaign of Christian bus ads he felt had been too fundamentalist. A total of 877 people pledged cash to the campaign.

The British Humanist Association then got involved and Richard Dawkins offered to match the first £5,500 of donations made to a JustGiving page that had been set up. The campaign appeal was widely reported because of its early success.

Word soon spread via social media and more than £150,000 was donated, wildly exceeding the expectations of everyone involved. It is perhaps one of the most successful viral marketing campaigns ever conducted.

(See Jon Worth's blog at **www.jonworth.eu**).

How journalists think and what they like to see

Journalists want to fill their publications with interesting news that is relevant to their readership and encouraging to their advertisers. The more specialist the publication, the more important it is that the content is specifically focused on the readership.

In general, journalists are looking for stories that are:

→ interesting – to current and potential readers;

→ exclusive – not available in any other publication (in the same form);

→ current – about something that is happening right now;

→ trendsetting – breaking new ground and potentially going to grow;

→ valuable – offering helpful advice to the readers.

Journalists also expect to be supplied with stories in a form that they can use. In other words, they prefer an emailed Word file or the text pasted into the body of an email so that it can be lifted out, edited and pasted into the publication. This is because most journalists also make up the pages of their publications or upload them on to the publication's website. By providing the text ready to paste, you are making life easier for them.

Do not underestimate the importance of submitting a well-presented, well-written news release accompanied by a professionally taken photograph. If your press release doesn't cover all that it should, it may not get used, as few journalists will have the time for further research.

Top Tip

For printed publications, photos need to be at a high resolution and submitted in JPEG format. As a rule of thumb, aim for a file size between 0.5 and 2Mb

A newspaper consists of just the same number of words, whether there be any news in it or not.

HENRY FIELDING

What journalists regard as news

News is all a matter of context. You might have won the biggest order of your life, but if last week's paper featured your competitor with an order ten times the size, your story will not be regarded as news.

If, on the other hand, you have just managed to persuade the producers of a TV soap opera to use your products as props in the programme, then however insignificant the order size, it will probably be regarded as news.

The difference is the involvement of the TV soap opera. All readers will be aware of it and many will watch it. Your ability to link the newspaper with the soap opera makes the story newsworthy.

Of course, the best way to find out what a journalist will regard as news is to pick up the phone and ask. In general, journalists on local newspapers or trade publications are receptive to phone calls from small business owners, particularly if they are brief and to the point. You won't find this works with the national press or with major consumer magazines.

As well as the obvious business successes, new appointments and significant investments that make up the bulk of business news releases, there are other topics that can get you into the media. For example:

→ your expert comment on a current hot topic ('Our new pregnancy app encourages mums to look after themselves better', says Dr Green of nutrition specialists Mummyvit.co.uk);

→ a high-profile event you are organising ('New York model Amy Buffer will be at Anytown boutique Charmers on XYZ to launch its new spring range');

→ 'how to' tips ('Ten top winter pruning tips by Adam Trimmer from Anytown Garden Centre');

→ human interest stories ('Manchester life coach Bertie Better to climb Kilimanjaro to raise money for leukaemia research');

→ volunteering opportunities ('Matron Mandy Morton is looking for volunteers to decorate her old folks' home, with paint and brushes donated by Brighton DIY store Colours').

Lifestyle	High growth
Usually, in a small business, what you do is more newsworthy than who you are. Unless, that is, you win a business award.	Fast-growing businesses are news in themselves. Publicise your success as people like doing business with successful businesses. Success breed success.

A few words about photographs

Often the make or break factor in getting your story into the media is your ability to provide a decent photograph. Each of the examples above stands a better chance of success if accompanied by professional photos – for example:

→ a shot of a pregnant woman with an iPad in a greengrocer's;

→ a shot of the New York model on the catwalk;

→ a picture of Adam pruning a shrub;

→ the life coach in full mountaineering gear on top of a Manchester landmark;

→ the old folks' home matron pointing out her tatty paintwork, paint and brush in hand.

Top Tip

Editors do not like pictures that are too promotional. Take shots that form a visual metaphor or are unusual and always include people.

The easy way to write a press release

Unless you have been invited to provide an article for a newspaper or magazine, you should aim to keep your press releases short. This makes it far easier for a journalist to see what your story is about. If you have a strong story, they will always come back to you for more information, but they prefer not to have to edit down a huge, multi-page release into the 100 or so words they have space for.

Press releases work best if they follow traditional and proven formula. Outlined below are the sections of the press release and how to cope with each of them. Let's use an example to illustrate the points. Imagine that you sell and install hot tubs. You have persuaded your supplier to write off an old model that has been in your showroom for a year and is slightly damaged. You have donated it to a local charity that works with disabled children.

Page header

It is always good to make it clear that your document is a press release. The way you do this is by:

→ printing 'News Release' in large type at the top;

→ adding 'For immediate release' unless for some special reason the story is not to be printed right away (some people use the word 'embargoed', which means hold until the date/time given);

→ adding the name, phone number and email address of the person the editor can contact for more details;

→ double-spacing the copy on the page so that it is easy to read and the journalists can insert their own notes;

→ using a clear typeface.

Headline

Your release should start with a headline. The chances are that a subeditor will rewrite a headline if the piece is printed, so focus your headline on impressing the journalist. Make it factual and don't worry if it runs to a couple of lines. For example, 'Donated hot tub provides splashing good fun at children's home.'

First paragraph

The opening paragraph needs to contain everything that you most want the publication to print. In many ways it should be a summary of the whole release. Try to add a quote, as this will be reproduced verbatim. In our story it might read like this:

Top Tubs, Newcastle's leading supplier of hot tubs and Jacuzzis, has just given a hot tub to The Pines home for children with disabilities. 'The children love splashing around in their new tub,' said home Director Zia Kapoor. 'What's more, playing in the jets of warm water really helps them as it soothes painful limbs and encourages them to gain greater mobility.'

The paragraph tells the reader that:

→ Top Tubs is generous and kind;

→ hot tubs are fun;

→ hot tubs are therapeutic and good for aching limbs.

Second paragraph

Next, you need to expand on the story and add some more information about both your company and your motivation. Reveal some of the reasons for doing what you do. In our example, the second paragraph might read:

Commenting on the donation, Top Tubs' proprietor Jane Smith said, 'I've always promoted hot tubs for their therapeutic benefits and because they can be a great place to relax with friends. One of our customers has a disabled child and told me how helpful the tub we sold them was. I wanted more children to have that same experience.'

This paragraph tells the reader that:

→ Jane listens to her customers;

→ she has a generous, caring nature;

→ hot tubs are great for relaxing.

Final paragraph

This is the paragraph that may or may not be included. Use it to provide supporting information and references, as well as more detail if appropriate. Make sure you do not miss out any basic information. A good way to test this is by checking that the five Ws of information are all included in the release somewhere: who, where, when, what and why. In the example, the final paragraph might read:

Recent research by leading disability charity XXXXXX showed that children with physical disabilities respond well to the soothing properties of warm water. It was reading a report of this research, as well as feedback from parents of a disabled child, that encouraged Jane Smith to make a generous gift to the children's home. The home is close to Top Tubs' showroom on XYZ Drive, Newcastle.

Mark that this is the end of the release with the word 'ENDS'.

Boilerplate

This is a summary of what your business is all about. It is your opportunity to tell what you do and when you were established, as well as a little more about yourself. It is where the journalist looks for additional material, such as the contact details of the best person to talk to for further information.

In the example above, the boilerplate could also contain hyperlinks to recent independent research that supports the claim children with physical disabilities benefit from using a hot tub.

| Top Tip |

If you are finding it hard to write your release, concentrate initially on the headline and first paragraph. Once this feels right, the rest will follow. Always set aside your work and read it afresh after a break, or ask someone else to check it, before you submit it to a journalist. You can't always see your own mistakes.

Dealing with bad news

Not all the news is good news. When your business faces a major problem that you suspect will be reported in the press, it is usually better for you to be the messenger. For example, if one of your customers suffered a serious injury using your product, or worse, on your premises, you may need to make a timely statement to the press in collaboration with your insurer. In some situations you may need to check your legal situation before doing this and, even if you have not used one before, a PR adviser can help you make sure you word your statement appropriately.

The alternative is that the media will report the story anyway. If you don't comment, they will say that you were 'not available for comment', or even 'refused to comment', either of which can have a negative impact on your image.

Case study
Heston Blumenthal, The Fat Duck,
www.thefatduck.co.uk

In February 2009 this Michelin-starred restaurant faced an unexpected challenge: 40 of the previous day's diners called to say they felt unwell. Rather than try to hide the story, Heston Blumenthal and his team went public, explaining in great detail all the steps they were taking to identify and solve the problem. They also closed for a few days until they could be confident all was well. Finally, those affected were offered a free return visit.

By responding quickly, openly and thoroughly to the problem, Blumenthal demonstrated clear commitment to customer safety. It was a one-off incident that could happen with any restaurant. The press were positive when they could have slated the chef and his business. He did the right thing and the restaurant's excellent reputation did not suffer at all.

If you are worried about the possibility of a negative story, seek confidential advice to draft a statement in advance just in case. This will help you to avoid saying the wrong thing under pressure and it could help to 'kill' the story in time if needed. If you don't want the journalist to come back to you, make sure 'No further comment will be issued at this time' is added at the end.

 Nothing travels faster than the speed of light with the possible exception of bad news, which obeys its own special laws. DOUGLAS ADAMS, *THE HITCHHIKER'S GUIDE TO THE GALAXY*

When to hire a PR agency and how to do it

PR agencies come in all shapes and sizes. It is important to get the right one if you want to publicise your business using professional help. Young businesses often overlook the power of PR, despite the fact that advertising can cost a lot more and achieve a lot less.

Just as you are starting your business, it can be very useful (and more economical) to work with a PR specialist who is also just starting a business.

Here are some of the advantages of using a PR consultant or agency:

→ they already know how to write effective news releases;

→ they will have a network of journalists they can talk to;

→ they may have other clients with whom you can collaborate;

→ they will have experience of damage limitation if things go wrong.

One of the best ways to find the right PR person is to ask the editors of the publications you want to be featured in to recommend someone. They will know who they like working with and who they find intensely annoying.

Frequently asked questions

Below are some of the types of concern new entrepreneurs have about dealing with PR.

Our local business magazine said they would only print our story if we buy advertising. What do you think we should do?
Quite a few small regional business magazines survive only because people pay to be featured in them. The trouble with this is that the reader knows the story is there because it has been paid for. A better choice is to seek an 'advertorial', where you pay for a promotional story to be written and published.

We had a celebrity open our shop and the local TV channel promised to come along but did not turn up. What did we do wrong?
You probably did nothing wrong. TV camera crews are very busy and if a bigger story breaks on the day, they always go there and give you a miss. Don't be disappointed if they don't show up – and don't stop trying.

You say that photographs are important but I hate having my photograph taken. Is it really that important?
You are the public face of your company and, as such, it is important that you are seen. Of all the challenges you face starting a business, getting used to having your photograph taken should be one of the smallest.

Key points

→ Editorial coverage is almost always more influential than advertising.

→ Don't overlook TV and radio. There are now hundreds of channels looking for content.

→ Good creative photography really pays off.

→ Bad news cannot be ignored.

Next step

Practise what you've read in this chapter on your family and friends. Become more persuasive and more confident at selling. Make selling fun.

_____

_____

_____

_____

Ways that anyone can be good at selling

Chapter Eighteen

Selling is not as difficult as you might first think. It is not about browbeating your prospect into submission. The most effective selling is simply having a structured conversation. Both of you want to explore the potential of doing business together.

Naturally your ambition is to get a sale. It should also be your prospect's ambition to make a purchase. If people are not interested in what you are selling, no amount of pressure or persuasion will change them. Equally, if you do not passionately believe that what you are selling is the right solution to your prospect's current challenge, it will show and you will lack credibility.

When you are selling your products or services, you are enthusing others about something you find very exciting. By selling what you do, you will share your vision and your dream, but it has to be their dream, too. Everyone is different, so their motivation for considering a purchase from you will be different from anyone else's. The structure of a sales interview enables you to understand those differences and demonstrate how you have the right solution.

If you are confident that what you are offering is of real value and you are committed to making it work, then you will be good at sales. Conversely, you can have all the sales techniques in the world but no faith in your product and you will fail.

 Do you want to spend the rest of your life selling sugared water or do you want a chance to change the world? STEVE JOBS (when recruiting a soft drinks executive to run Apple)

A few words about buying

In Chapter Fifteen you were introduced to the concept of buying motives. These are the reasons that people buy anything. Your product or service has to satisfy one or more of the following needs: security, performance, appearance, convenience, economy and durability (remember the SPACED mnemonic). The buyer may not feel motivated to make a purchase right now, but they will be aware that they have a need. For example:

How to Start Your Own Business for Entrepreneurs

→ the works manager knows that they really must get round to updating the company's health and safety policies;

→ the householder with rotten windows knows that sometime soon they must buy replacements;

→ the 80-year-old widower knows that keeping his house clean is becoming more of a challenge every week and that soon he must find a cleaner.

What each of these people lacks is the sense of urgency that will lead them to make their decision immediately. They know that they have a need. However, the need is not yet pressing enough for them to go out and look for a solution. What they need help with is deciding to do something about it now.

Case study

Ian Pocock, Peak Electromagnetics,
www.peak-em.co.uk

A chartered engineer, Ian Pocock established Peak Electromagnetics in 2004. The company provides comprehensive support to manufacturers, reliably and effectively taking their products from concept through to testing.

Before starting his own business, Ian had been providing consultancy services as an employee, so he was accustomed to managing his time and projects. However, selling himself was something he'd not done before.

'Most of the information I could find was helpful for people selling products, not services,' he explained. 'I found **www.shout99.com**, a UK freelancers' online network, to be a really helpful source of practical advice.'

Lifestyle	High growth
However much you might not feel confident selling, it really is a skill every business owner has to master. We all have to sell all of the time.	As well as being able to sell, when your business grows quickly you also need to be able to manage salespeople. This is a different skill (see **www.ismm.co.uk**).

The sales process, step by step

When you start a sales conversation, both parties will know that you are about to talk business. That does not mean you have to start talking formally or use different words. It means you have to take control of the conversation and gently steer it along a logical path. That logical path can be defined in the following way.

Preparation

Before you start your sales conversation, make sure you have prepared fully. This is your business now and your prospective new customer will expect you to know the answers and be able to make decisions.

You prepare for a sales conversation by:

→ being familiar with what you are trying to sell;

→ knowing exactly what deal you can strike and still make a profit;

→ having checked out your prospect and having some idea about what might motivate them to buy (although you will not have a closed mind);

→ checking that the person you are talking to has the authority to make the purchase – for example, at home the customer will usually want to ask their partner before committing; at work the person you are talking to might have the authority to agree the specification but lack the budgetary responsibility to make the actual purchase.

Approach

Next, you need to get your prospect's attention and start a conversation. If you are meeting somebody by appointment this is not a problem. If they have walked into your shop and are looking intently at a particular product, then it can be difficult to know how to go about starting a conversation. The same is true if you are at an exhibition and somebody comes to your stand or perhaps just pauses in the aisle to read one of your displays. You can make your approach and break the ice by:

→ walking into their field of vision (rather than creeping up from behind);

→ asking what interests them about whatever it is they are looking at;

→ introducing yourself and paying them an appropriate compliment;

→ smiling.

Top Tip

If you don't know the answer to something your prospect asks, say so and promise to find out. Never bluff because then everything you say will seem to be bluff. It's OK to call the office or even a supplier to check something during a sales meeting.

Exploring the customer's needs

Once you have broken the ice and started a conversation you need to take it somewhere constructive. You do that by asking questions that will help you understand the customer's needs and motivation. The context within which the conversation takes place will help you to start. For example, in a shop or at an exhibition, finding out how, where and why they might use whatever it is you are displaying is a natural place to go. If you are meeting them by appointment they will expect to be asked questions that relate to your products or services.

Top Tip

If you get stuck, ask your prospect a question. One that works for me is, 'I feel I'm not quite telling you what you need to know to make your decision. What's bothering you about XYZ?' The answer will take you closer to a sale!

Remember

Open questions usually include the words who, what, where, why and when. They encourage the other person to open up and share information. **Closed questions** usually demand a short answer, often yes or no. They are used to check understanding and gain commitment.

In a sales conversation you will use open questions to learn more about the other person and what interests them. When you want to change direction or focus them on a particular aspect of what they have said you use a closed question to stop the flow and take them in the direction you want to go. Use open questions to go faster and closed questions to slow down. Vary the speed according to the route you're taking.

Presenting your solution

Having worked out the other person's needs (that you can meet), it is time to suggest your solution. You start by summarising what it is you think your prospect wants and why. Use a closed question to get them to confirm that this is the case or to tell you more if you have not quite got it right.

Then, using a phrase such as 'Let me tell you about XYZ', you can present your solution to their need. When describing benefits you can offer, place the greatest emphasis on those most relevant to their need. In other words, put aside your own views about what is most important and concentrate instead on theirs.

 In the factory we make cosmetics; in the drugstore we sell hope. CHARLES REVSON

Getting commitment

Now that you have identified your customer's need and explained why your product or service solves the problem, it is time to get commitment. It is human nature to put off making a commitment and your job is to stop that happening.

The art of getting commitment is to make it as easy as possible for the other person to say yes. You can do this by:

→ summarising the argument for purchase and then asking for the order;

→ breaking down the deal and committing them to one piece at a time, building up to a whole;

How to Start Your Own Business for Entrepreneurs

→ offering them two alternatives, both of which involve saying yes –
for example, 'Would you like it delivered on Tuesday or some time
next week?'

> ### Top Tip
>
> Of all sales techniques, the 'alternative close' is the easiest to get the hang
> of as well as the most successful way to get commitment. The key (as
> illustrated above) is to offer one very specific alternative (Tuesday) and a
> less specific alternative (some time next week).
> If 'some time next week' is chosen you simply say, 'Thank you for saying
> yes; now which day next week works best for you?'

If you have found out enough to really understand the customer's
need and have presented your case clearly, getting commitment
should happen naturally. If you meet resistance you have not done
your job properly.

Overcoming objections

Inevitably, there will be some barriers to saying yes straight away.
Asking for commitment is a good way to identify what the sticking
points are. When your prospect says no, you need to find out why. You
do this by saying something like:

→ 'Could you tell me what it is you're not yet sure about?'

→ 'From our conversation I thought you could see why this is a good
move for you. What is holding you back?'

Sometimes there might be a very good reason why the person is
unable to place an order at that time. When this happens you have to
arrange to get back in touch when they are ready.

Once you are working through the objections and dealing with them
one by one, you are at the most focused stage of the sales interview.
Your conversation will cycle between dealing with objections and seeking
commitment. Your goal is to gain some commitment if not the order.

If you try too hard to get commitment (called 'closing the deal'), you risk alienating your prospect. You have to watch their body language and listen to what they say to decide when the time has come to call a halt. What is important is that you leave the meeting with some commitment, even if it is only to talk again in a month or two.

Case study

David Aldridge, Herne Bay Mobility,
www.hernebaymobility.co.uk

Redundancy from a senior management position gave David Aldridge the push he needed to start Herne Bay Mobility. Most of his customers are elderly and, as he told me, 'are not a group of people to hard sell to.' That said, he does believe in being professional. 'Selling skills are essential,' he says. 'However, if it is the right product for the customer and the quality and price are good, then 75 per cent of your job is done for you.'

Something of a computer enthusiast, David conducts much of his business online, where it is even more important to play it straight. Amazon and eBay, for example, have strict rules for traders and your reputation depends on positive customer feedback.

David is successful because he knows both how to sell and when to simply let the customers make the decision for themselves.

In their second year of trading, Herne Bay Mobility came second in a local 'Small Business of the Year' competition, winning £1,500 worth of free advertising, and expanded into larger premises. The recruitment of an experienced engineer added another string to their bow by enabling them to become insurance-approved repairers. Now they can offer a full service and repair package to their customers.

How to get lasting commitment

Few businesses seek to sell to each customer only once. It is far easier to get repeat business or recommendations from your existing customers than to recruit and convert new ones. As you become established you should find that an increasing proportion of your turnover comes from repeat or introduced business. This makes life far easier and more pleasant as you are dealing with people you know.

Repeat orders and recommendations do not happen spontaneously. You have to nurture them by building a lasting and meaningful relationship with your customer. This starts the moment they agree to the first transaction.

It is important that you confirm in writing, perhaps via email, what was agreed when you closed the sale. You can use the same communication to reinforce the positive reasons why the customer has bought from you. You can also make the point that you grow your business by recommendation and would love to meet anyone your customer feels might be interested in what you have to offer.

Good ways to keep in touch and build your relationship with your customers include:

→ regular newsletters and updates that offer useful information, not just sales messages;

→ proactive customer service, including courtesy calls to check that all is well and sales calls at around the time the customer is likely to be buying more;

→ incentives to introduce new customers or try new products/ services;

→ encouraging them to sponsor various charitable activities you might engage in – for example, you might run a marathon to raise money for your local hospice.

Keeping track of your sales leads

As your business grows you will gain more and more customers. You will also find that you have an increasing number of prospects, some lukewarm and some quite hot. It can be difficult to keep track of when you have promised to get back to people and what you have been talking about.

Most people find it helpful to use what is called CRM software. CRM stands for 'Customer Relationship Management'. There are several on the market to choose from, none too expensive for the start-up business.

Top Tip

Sign up with a CRM website. It can give you the discipline you need to keep on top of your growing pool of prospects and prompt you when the time is right to contact people.

Frequently asked questions

Here are some typical questions that new entrepreneurs ask about sales.

We sell and lay brick-paved drives and patios. The problem we have is that although people love the product and seem happy with the price, they always want to put off doing the job until later. How can we get commitment from people to do something now?

You need to create a sense of urgency and take away some of the pain of the big invoice when the job is finished. I suspect you would also benefit from being able to schedule your work more effectively, so that you lay patios when it suits you rather than being very busy and then very quiet. You need to break the year into campaigns and then have a different incentive to purchase for each campaign. For example, you might offer spread payments so that customers can have the patio now and pay over three months. You might also offer free extras such as drain covers (if the full order is placed and paid for by a particular date) at certain times of the year.

▶

I am not a salesperson by any stretch of the imagination. Why can't I just hire someone to do the selling for me?

Talking to your prospective customers will teach you more about what your business needs to do to succeed than anything else. You cannot afford to delegate all your sales activity to other people unless you want to risk losing touch with what your business really does.

We have a shop and I find it really difficult to break the ice and start conversations. I find myself saying silly things like, 'Can I help you?' Can you help me?

Perhaps your shop layout makes it difficult to saunter up to people and start a conversation. Would it help if you arranged things differently? You might also try offering samples if that is appropriate or even saying that you are conducting a survey to find out what people think of a particular product. In many ways it doesn't matter where you start, you just need to start!

Key points

→ Make sure the person you are speaking to has the authority and need to buy.

→ A sales conversation should feel natural and be enjoyed by both parties.

→ Practise following the sales sequence in this chapter and make it second nature.

→ Invest in software that will help you to keep in touch with your prospects.

→ Do not take it personally when people say no – they are rejecting the offer and not you.

Next step

Work out the benefits you think your products or services offer, then try to sell them to someone you know will give you honest feedback.

_____

_____

_____

_____

Reputation – making friends and influencing people

Chapter Nineteen

Good news spreads fast, particularly if you encourage it. Chapter Seventeen looked at how PR can help you build a good reputation, but what exactly is reputation and how can you influence it? In a world where products and services are all pretty much the same, your reputation and what you stand for will increasingly make all the difference.

Online marketplaces such as eBay measure reputation. People will use your reputation rating to decide if they want to do business with you. The traders on eBay work hard to maintain a high reputation rating. These ratings are based on the speed with which you dispatch goods that have been ordered from you and how well you handle any disputes.

In the face-to-face business world, as opposed to online, reputation is more complex. However, as with the eBay reputation rating, it is what you do and how you do it that will dictate how good your reputation is in your marketplace.

> ## You can't build a reputation on what you are going to do. HENRY FORD

What is reputation and why is it important?

When Gerald Ratner was quoted out of context for describing his company's products as 'crap', his company soon went out of business. The inference was that he was exploiting his customers by selling them cheap tat. Even now, 20 years later (he made the famous speech in 1991), he is still trying to live down that moment. It did massive damage to his entrepreneurial career.

Sir Richard Branson, on the other hand, has a consistently good reputation for challenging a marketplace, by introducing competition to reduce prices and improve the customer deal. The image of this successful entrepreneur as a man unafraid of a challenge is reinforced by some of his well-publicised adventures. Yet he too has had failures along the way; we just don't hear about them as we did with Ratner.

Reputation is, by definition, just an opinion. It is an opinion formed by those around you – in this context, your potential customers. Opinions are not necessarily based on actual knowledge, but more often on hearsay and anecdotal evidence.

Lifestyle	High growth
Reputation is equally important with any size of organisation. If you run the local pub and lose your good name, it's difficult to entice people from further away to patronise your business.	Just as Ratner was toppled by a misquoted speech, so too can something seemingly small wreck the reputation of a growing business. If you lead a growing firm, remember that personal reputation can impact your businesses success.

Case study
Bláithín O'Reilly Murphy, The Wedding Expert,
www.blaithinoreillymurphy.com

Bláithín O'Reilly Murphy tried lots of careers, including working as an interior designer and air hostess, before setting up as a wedding consultant in 2007. It seemed to be a service that encompassed much of what she'd most enjoyed doing up until then. Most of all, she wanted the freedom of being her own boss.

Much of her work comes by word of mouth, so reputation is vital. A wedding magazine editor suggested she write a book. *Distinctive Weddings: Tying the Knot without the Rope Burns!* was published in 2008 (Veritas) and she tells me she is 'the first Irish wedding planner to have written [a book] for the Irish market'. She is now approached whenever journalists want a comment on weddings. She is also in talks with a production company about a possible TV show.

By building her reputation in this way, her popularity as a wedding consultant has grown and her business future is assured.

How to build and maintain your reputation

The best way to build your business reputation is to exceed people's expectations. However, you also have to do this without exceeding your own budget. You have to be able to both wow people and be profitable.

Here are some simple ways a business can build its reputation.

→ Answering the phone quickly and responding to all enquiries promptly.

→ Always being helpful, polite and knowledgeable.

→ Setting and beating realistic deadlines. In other words, if you expect to deliver the goods on Wednesday, promise delivery on Thursday to give yourself some leeway. Then, when you deliver on Wednesday, you look very efficient.

→ Being more than fair when dealing with product returns or customer complaints. It is often better to bend to meet the demands of the slightly unrealistic complainant than suffer the consequences of them bad-mouthing you all around the neighbourhood.

→ Associating yourself and your business with worthwhile causes and projects. Be careful not to let these take over your life, but giving a small part of your profits to a local charity will work wonders for your business reputation (and probably give you a better return on investment than some other forms of marketing).

In a world where the internet can reveal some of the most intimate details of our personal lives to anyone caring to look, reputations built at work can be shattered at home. Of course, you cannot realistically live every moment as if your business depended on it, but you can consider the potential business consequences before, for example, having a rant on a social networking site on a Saturday afternoon.

Top Tip

Always, always under-promise and over-deliver. Give yourself some leeway and then more often than not you can exceed your customers' expectations. People remember excellence!

How your reputation can work for you

A good reputation does much more for your business than simply win you more customers. Reputation can be reflected in the value of your business, listed on the balance sheet as 'goodwill' (see next section).

Another word for reputation is popularity. When you are popular, people want to be with you. In a business context this may be reflected in the following ways.

→ People will like doing business with you. This means greater customer loyalty and customers who will tell you if you need to change your offer to stay in the market.

→ Suppliers will want to help you succeed. This means being supplied ahead of less popular rivals in times of scarcity and perhaps even some leniency if you need longer to pay now and again.

→ Employees will be more enthusiastic and less likely to leave. Your workforce will also be willing to do that little bit extra because they will have bought into your vision for the business.

→ Neighbours will be more tolerant, for example, if they are frequently asked to sign for deliveries when you are out or if at times your business makes a lot of noise or takes up a lot of parking at a business centre.

Case study
Lesley Morgan, Hotel Indigo, Glasgow,
www.hotelindigo.com

Hotel Indigo Glasgow is one of a small network of branded boutique hotels within the global Intercontinental Hotel group. Although part of a major corporate, each hotel is managed as a unique local business.

Reputation management is important for any business, but vital for a hotel. Guest reviews on Trip Advisor can make or break a hotel, so making sure guests are happy and any concerns are quickly dealt with is very important.

Lesley goes one step further than most. She checks Trip Advisor most days and posts a response to every review of her hotel. This does two things. First, it demonstrates that she takes criticism seriously and also appreciates praise. Second, people will be less likely to post an unfairly negative review if they know it will be responded to by the hotel.

It is no surprise that, on Trip Advisor, Hotel Indigo is the best-rated hotel in Glasgow!

Reputation and your business' value

When you look at a large company's balance sheet you will sometimes see a value attributed to 'goodwill'. Goodwill is used to describe reputation in monetary terms.

Building goodwill can be very important if you want to sell your business at some time in the future. For example, take two identical window cleaning companies. Both employ five people and both have annual sales of £300,000. The owners both want to sell their businesses at the same time.

Here are some facts about business A:

→ it has a reputation for cutting corners and skimping on jobs when under pressure;

→ the workforce do not take pride in their work and there have been complaints that they loiter and smoke outside customers' premises;

→ the workforce are paid little above minimum wage and enjoy few work benefits;

→ by keeping overheads very low, business is more profitable.

Here are some facts about business B:

→ it gives its regular customers flowers at Christmas and always phones to check if it is convenient before arriving to clean windows;

→ it takes staff off the road one day a month for customer care training and teambuilding days;

→ it pays its workforce a fair basic wage plus bonuses when they achieve productivity targets;

→ it is less profitable than business A.

When the owners started to market their businesses, potential buyers understandably wanted reassurance that the customers would remain loyal to the new firm, as would the workforce. They wanted things to continue very much as before and would be relying on the goodwill of the customer base to maintain the business and generate the income needed to buy out the existing owners.

If you were buying one of these two businesses, which would you choose?

There is no doubt in my mind that you would buy business B and set out to poach customers from business A as the easy way to grow the business further.

You earn reputation by trying to do hard things well. JEFF BEZOS

Frequently asked questions

Here are some questions that new entrepreneurs have asked with regard to reputation.

I started my business after leaving prison and coming off drugs. How can I possibly build a good reputation when people know about my past?
It is the fact you have changed your life in such a dramatic way that will make you popular and build your reputation. We cannot change the past but we can certainly change the future. Many in your situation would have taken the easier path and not started a business. People will respect you for that.

We provide domiciliary care services to the elderly and, whatever we do to please them, they are, by their very nature, grumpy and unappreciative at times. I think we go well beyond what is expected but I don't think this group of customers realises that. How can we build our reputation?

▶

I would argue that the people you need to influence in terms of reputation are not the elderly themselves, but their friends and family who, but for you, would be the ones caring for them. Why not start sending regular updates and information to the next of kin of those you care for? It is these people who will be recommending you to others with aged parents needing care.

I have no intention of ever selling my business, so adding value in terms of goodwill does not appeal as much as making a bigger profit right now. Am I wrong?

I would say that you are not wrong but short-sighted. Just suppose you want to borrow money in the future. Would your bank not prefer to lend to someone with a great reputation, rather than to a business that milks every opportunity for as much as it can get?

Another aspect of starting a business that some entrepreneurs find daunting is handling finances. In the next chapter you'll discover how to make the process relatively painless.

Key points

You build a good reputation by:

→ being firm but fair;

→ exceeding expectations;

→ playing an active role in the wider world;

→ being honest;

→ being profitable so that you can continue to build your reputation.

Next step

Be honest with yourself and plan your business around you, your strengths and your vision for your future.

_____

_____

_____

_____

Managing your business

Part Four

How to do your bookkeeping without tears

Chapter Twenty

You can look on keeping the books as a chore – or you can learn how keeping your finger on your business' pulse can be both enjoyable and informative. One thing is certain; you cannot ignore the financial performance of your business.

Many people use a freelance bookkeeper to do their basic bookkeeping, calculate VAT returns and prepare the monthly payroll.

Others prefer to do these tasks themselves, recognising that it is not difficult to keep the books straight in a relatively uncomplicated start-up business. You may surprise yourself when you find out how little time it can take to do the paperwork if you start out with a good, simple system.

In this world nothing can be said to be certain, except death and taxes. BENJAMIN FRANKLIN

Why is bookkeeping so important?

There is no law that says you have to keep any records at all, unless you are trading as a limited company or registered charity, in which case you are legally bound to prepare accounts. Most business start-ups are either sole traders or partnerships and as such their annual tax bill is calculated from their annual tax return.

To complete your tax return you need accurate records of your income and expenditure. You must be able to back up your tax return with documentary evidence should the tax authorities want to check. Therefore, it makes sense to keep comprehensive records of your business transactions and keep these totally separate from your personal finances.

If you have previously been employed, you will be familiar with having your tax and National Insurance deducted from your pay before you receive it. Now that you have your own business, you will pay a flat rate of National Insurance and your income tax twice a year, in January and July. Your employer will have been responsible for calculating these deductions. Now that you are your own employer, it is your responsibility. That is another good reason for keeping accurate accounts.

If you have always been employed, you may not have been asked to complete a tax return. Because, as an entrepreneur, your income and expenditure are more complex, HM Revenue & Customs (HMRC) give you a tax return on which to provide them with the details they need. You complete your tax returns online.

Top Tip

Most bookkeeping software allows for complexity. You should aim for simplicity. You can always build in more detail later as your enterprise grows.

What do you do first?

When you decide to start your own business it is important to take as much advice as possible. Remember that the tax authorities are there to help you get things right, as well as to collect tax from you.

Here are some important first steps to take when you start your business.

→ Contact HMRC (**www.hmrc.gov.uk**), the UK government department that deals with personal tax and National Insurance. Use your latest tax office reference number to locate the right office and let it know that you are starting your own business. The website has some useful downloads and it can offer advice.

→ If you expect your turnover to exceed £73,000 in the first year you might choose to register for VAT straight away. This is handled by a separate department within HMRC. Again, the website contains a lot of useful information. Note that you do not have to register until the quarter after which your turnover exceeds the registration threshold.

→ Contact your insurance broker if you are going to be using your car for business purposes or if you are going to work from home. There is a risk that if you do not inform your insurance company and have a claim relating to your business activities it might refuse to pay out. You will also need public liability insurance, which is very cheap to obtain, but let your broker advise you.

→ Open a business bank account. Most banks have new business starter packs and offer at least 12 months' free banking. Don't automatically go to the bank you use personally; often it is a good idea to keep your business and personal finances completely separate.

Lifestyle	High growth
It's never too early in your enterprise's life for you to get your bookkeeping organised. The easier you make this, the more time you have for more interesting stuff!	Scrupulous record keeping is vital for the growing business for two reasons. First, rapid growth can squeeze cash flow so you need a finger on the pulse of the business. Second, it makes due diligence far easier when you come to sell.

What records should you keep?

Your business' bank statements and a written record (supported by invoices and receipts) of each transaction is essentially all you need to have. When the time comes to submit your tax return you will need this information to complete the form.

You also need to keep a record of any other expenses you have incurred in the course of your business that can be allowed against your trading income. These may not all be transactions made through a business account because some of your domestic bills may be allowable. For example, if you are self-employed or in a partnership and work from home you may be able to claim:

→ a proportion of your home heating and electricity bills;

→ some of your mortgage interest;

→ your broadband subscription;

→ other expenses directly linked to your business.

In addition, if you use your car for work, you can offset most of the running costs and depreciation within certain limits.

My money goes to my agent, then to my accountant and from him to the tax man.

GLENDA JACKSON

Simple systems to make life easier

With more than 300,000 people starting a business in the UK every year, it is not surprising that there are some very efficient bookkeeping software packages on the market. They are affordable and some can be upgraded to more sophisticated versions as your business grows.

Some, such as Sage Instant (**http://shop.sage.co.uk/instantaccounts. aspx**), Quickbooks (**www.intuit.co.uk/quickbooks/accounting-software/ index.jsp**), and Cashflow Manager (**www.cashflow-manager.co.uk**), come on a CD with a handbook to get you started. Others, such as Kashflow (**www.kashflow.co.uk**), are web-based and you pay a monthly subscription.

If you are using an accountant to prepare annual accounts and complete your tax returns (which usually proves to be a sound investment), use a software package they recommend. You can then simply email them your accounts as an attachment and they can open it at their end to check your figures.

Case study

Pauline X

Pauline's company works in a highly sensitive, professional marketplace where confidentiality is of paramount importance. While asking to remain anonymous, she is willing to share her experience of choosing accounting software.

'We work to very tight client deadlines and without professional accounting software or experience, neither of us felt able to devote sufficient time to the accounting side of the company and accounts were compiled, out of necessity, at the end of the financial year and passed to our accountant,' she explained.

'I don't remember exactly how I came across Kashflow, but I was intrigued by the accessibility and potential ease of use of their software.' Pauline was offered a month's free trial and quickly found that 'the software quickly improved our business and was essential in retaining information for our accountants on a monthly and annual basis'.

'As owners of a fast-growing small business, the ease of use – and professional invoices produced – transformed what could have been a long-winded, boring and easily avoidable process into a pleasant, rewarding and easy strand of business practice.'

(See **www.kashflow.com** for more information).

Understanding the jargon

When you are new to entrepreneurship, the terminology and jargon used by accountants and bank managers can seem daunting. Here are some of the words you will encounter, explained in everyday language.

Assets: things (usually physical) your business owns that have a financial value.

Liabilities: the general term embracing all your business owes.

Long-term liabilities: usually debts that are not yet due for repayment in total – for example, mortgages and business loans.

Short-term liabilities: the things you have to pay for soon.

Debtors: the term used to describe people who owe you money – in other words, customers who have been invoiced but have not yet paid.

Creditors: the people who have invoiced you and you have not yet paid.

Balance sheet: literally balances your assets and liabilities and calculates the net value of your business. On one side it totals your physical assets and debtors and on the other your total liabilities including creditors. The balance sheet will show long-term liabilities separately because, although they affect the value of the business, they are not due for payment yet and will contribute to future income.

Profit and loss account: this year's trading performance over a period of time, arrived at by comparing your income with your payments. As your business grows you will find it useful to prepare a monthly profit and loss account so you can see that everything is on track.

Income and expenditure: income from sales and costs incurred.

Cash flow: the flow of money in and out of your business. Sometimes people talk about a positive cash flow; this is where you receive payment for something before you have had to pay your suppliers. For example, a fish and chip shop will pay for its potatoes a month after delivery. People buying fish and chips pay straight away, so you have been paid for the potatoes before you have to pay for them.

Gross margin: your selling price less the costs directly attributable to that sale, such as materials.

Overheads: business costs that cannot directly be attributed to a specific sale – for example, labour, rent and finance costs.

Bottom line: your net profit.

Finding time

Doing the books need not be an arduous task. Once you have set up your accounting software with headings that suit your business, it should take you no more than a couple of hours a month to keep your books up to date.

It is always good practice to complete your bookkeeping soon after the end of each month. This will give you a good feel for how your business is doing and enable you to spot any errors you might have missed during the month.

If you have a book-keeping system that does not record each invoice as it is raised, but, rather, when it is paid, you also need to make time to check through your file of unpaid invoices so that any now-overdue payments can be chased up.

> **Top Tip**
>
> Do your monthly accounts early in the next month so that any errors can be quickly spotted and corrected.

How to choose the right accountant

Choosing an accountant is like buying shoes for a child. You are looking for a comfortable fit and also room for growth. However, buy shoes that are too large or too small and they will be uncomfortable to wear and possibly damage your feet.

Accountants, like shoes, come in many shapes and sizes. An accountancy practice that works with major corporations is unlikely to be the right one for a start-up business, unless that start-up business is quickly going to become a major corporation.

The best accountants win new clients by recommendation. You can short-cut this process by asking people you know and respect if they would recommend their accountant to you. Like doctors, accountants are very strict about client confidentiality and will never discuss your business with another client. Look for an accountant who:

→ you can relate to as a person;

→ understands your business sector;

→ is enthusiastic about your new enterprise;

→ has recognised accountancy qualifications;

→ appreciates that as a start-up you have a limited budget.

Frequently asked questions

The following are some typical questions that new entrepreneurs have about book-keeping and accountants.

I started my business last year and was shocked at the size of my accountant's invoice when she prepared my first year's accounts. I had done my own book-keeping but the bill was still larger than I had expected. Is this normal?

There are two things to comment on here. First, it will always cost more for your accountant to deal with your first year's trading as you both are doing things for the first time. Ask for an estimate of next year's costs so that you do not get an unpleasant surprise. Second, many accountants are happy for clients to pay their fee by instalments throughout the year. This helps their cash flow as well as yours.

I have found an accountant I would like to use and they have suggested doing everything for me, including preparing management accounts. All I have to do is drop in the copy invoices and bills every month and they will do the rest. This sounds good – what do you think?

I think this sounds expensive and, unless you are completely daunted by the prospect of doing any of it yourself, I would advise against outsourcing everything. As your business grows, you will spot things while doing your monthly accounts that the professionals might miss.

A friend I play golf with tells me that he takes most of his income from his business as dividends. What does this mean and should I be doing the same?

When you have a limited liability company (Ltd), the profits can be distributed to the shareholders as dividends. These are taxed differently from the salary your friend will be taking through the year. In some situations, accountants advise clients with limited companies to take most of their income as dividends, as this can mean a lower tax bill.

When you are keeping current with your accounts, you will always know how large your profits are. Of course, you will always want them to be larger – and that is the topic of the next chapter.

Key points

→ Tell the tax authorities when you are starting your business and seek their help in getting things organised.

→ Keep your business and personal finances completely separate.

→ Find a good accountant to deal with your tax affairs.

Next step

Take a look at a number of bookkeeping software systems. Compare benefits and choose one that is simple enough to understand and detailed enough to give you the information you need.

_____

_____

_____

_____

How to make your profits bigger

Chapter Twenty-one

A popular adage used by business advisers is to say that 'turnover is vanity and profit is sanity'. The saying is popular because, too often, people starting and growing a business focus on increasing their sales turnover without paying due regard to profitability.

Of course, you need a level of turnover to cover your overhead costs, but in nine out of ten businesses, the best way to make more money is to improve the profitability, not increase the turnover. This is because more sales mean more production, which means more overheads and more costs. If you can increase the profitability of your existing turnover, nothing changes apart from the bottom line.

Naturally, your customers will not simply volunteer to give you a greater margin on the business you do together. You cannot just reduce the specification and quality of what you do and expect to retain the same price. This will not please your customers. Instead, you have to add value so that your customers are happy to do business with you and willingly pay a premium price for a premium service.

 ## If you mean to profit, learn to please.

WINSTON CHURCHILL

What is the difference between turnover and profit?

Imagine for a moment that you run a boarding kennels. People leave their dogs with you when they go away on holiday or are temporarily unable to care for their pet at home. You charge your customers on a per dog per day basis.

The amount of food a dog eats, not surprisingly, depends on its size. A big dog will eat three times as much food as a small dog. Both dogs occupy the same space and take the same amount of time to look after. So, the more small dogs you have in your kennels, the more profitable your business is because you are buying less food – as the following illustration shows.

How to Start Your Own Business for Entrepreneurs

Twenty dogs 'paying' £50 per week gives you a weekly turnover of £1,000. Your average weekly costs are as follows:

Labour	£500
Materials	£100
Food	£200
Total	**£800**

Therefore, your profit is £1,000 – £800 = £200, or 20 per cent of turnover.

Now, you have noticed that when you have a lot of large dogs, your food bill goes up to £250 a week. If you have a lot of small dogs it drops to £150 a week. In other words, if you have a lot of large dogs, your weekly profit can fall to £150 and if you have a lot of small dogs, it can rise to £250. Multiply this by 50 weeks in the year (as you'll need some holiday) and the potential additional profit from housing only small dogs is £5,000.

The way to make more profit from the same turnover with this business is to specialise in catering for the needs of small dogs. You might find that owners of small dogs are different from owners of large dogs, so you might focus your marketing on meeting the needs of the owners of small dogs.

To look at this another way, you would need to extend your kennels to accommodate more dogs and possibly hire in more labour if you wanted to make the same additional profit by catering for large dogs. Focusing on increasing profit rather than turnover dramatically reduces your need for investment and the risk associated with seeking additional customers.

Now look and see how you can apply the same principle to your business.

Top Tip

It is almost always the case that your more profitable customers will give you less hassle than those who contribute little to your bottom line. Be very good at what you do and discerning when it comes to pitching for new business.

Why will some deals always make more than others?

Some deals will always make more money than others. For one thing, when you first start your business you will almost inevitably be so enthusiastic to get some sales you will do deals that in the future you would not consider worthwhile. The challenge there is to move away from those unprofitable customers as soon as you can.

As a rule of thumb, the more value you add to your customer's life or business, the more they will pay for what you do. For example, a graphic designer creating a full-page advertisement will be able to charge a higher fee to a large company placing this in a national publication than to a small company placing a similar ad in a local newspaper. This is because the ad in the national publication has potential to make much more money for the advertiser. Both adverts probably take the same amount of time and effort to create.

The more value you add, the more the customer will pay. Value is different from cost! Generally, you will be able to make higher profits from deals that are done with the following customers.

→ Larger customers with the potential to place bigger orders. They often take less time to make up their minds than people placing small orders.

→ People who themselves run successful organisations or have high personal income. They will be able to work out the return they will get on their investment in your business.

→ Organisations where the positive impact of your work can be large. These will also be quicker decision-makers than people for whom the purchase is not crucial to their short-term success.

→ People with a problem that needs fixing quickly. For example, repairs on oil rigs where every hour of lost production means a huge financial loss to the rig operator.

Generally, you will make smaller profits from deals that are done with the following customers.

→ People with limited budgets who have to make every penny count.

→ Individuals who do not value their own time and will be unlikely to value yours.

→ Organisations where the benefit you can deliver is marginal.

→ People with problems that will only slowly get worse. For example, persuading a restaurant owner to replace worn flooring will not be easy until it becomes dangerous. The disruption of replacing it will encourage the restaurateur to put off repair as long as possible.

> **Top Tip**
>
> The 80/20 rule applies here as much as anywhere else: 20 per cent of your customers will give you 80 per cent of your profit. Do not allow yourself to be distracted by the 80 per cent of your customers who together only give you 20 per cent of your profit. Always focus on the most lucrative customers.

The successful man will profit from his mistakes and try again in a different way. DALE CARNEGIE

How to work out your profitability

You will only know which of your transactions are the most profitable if you measure your profitability deal by deal. This is easy if you are selling your time as a self-employed consultant. Your costs will remain largely the same irrespective of the daily fee you charge your client. Therefore the higher the day rate you charge, the more profitable the client becomes for you.

If you make or sell products, your profitability can be harder to work out. You have to produce enough sales to cover your overhead costs. For instance, if you have an ice-cream van and park beside the beach, you must sell enough ice-cream to cover the cost of the van before you make any money for yourself. You might calculate your profitability like this.

Ice-cream van cost you £10,000 and will last 5 years	£2,000 p.a.
Running costs, fuel, repairs and insurance	£2,000 p.a.
Total running costs	£4,000 p.a.
Trading days (summer and weekends)	200
Income needed to cover overheads	£200/day

You buy ice-creams for £1 each and sell them for £2. You have to sell 200 ice-creams a day to cover your overheads and reach break-even point. After you have sold your first 200 ice-creams, you know that you are making £1 per ice-cream for yourself.

However, if you are the only ice-cream van on the beach and the weather is hot, you can sell at a higher price as people are otherwise faced with a long walk. This means you need to sell fewer units to cover your daily overheads and start making money sooner.

The key to calculating your profitability is knowing:

→ what your overhead costs are;

→ what your buying price is for products and raw materials;

→ what costs are incurred in processing, preparing and packing (as these can be easily overlooked);

→ what the market price is so that you are not selling too cheaply.

Lifestyle	High growth
Remember that the more profitable you make each transaction the fewer transactions you need to live well.	Cash flow always gets squeezed when a business grows quickly. You need to increase the profitability of each transaction to reduce the risk of running out of cash.

Case study
Jonny White, Zimma Web Development, www.zimma.co.uk

By the time Jonny White graduated with a software engineering degree, he had already established a thriving business building and maintaining websites. He enjoyed the work and charged what seemed like a lot of money at the time: £9 per hour.

As his workload grew he realised he could not afford to take on staff and continue to make a profit. He had to either increase his prices or turn work away.

His customers had also been telling him he was too cheap, so when Jonny increased his prices, he kept most of his customers and was able to employ an assistant. His business began to grow. He now has time to set aside to plan his future. As he said to me, 'I now feel I'm running my business rather than my business running me.'

How to add extra profit without really trying

There are two ways to add profit to each deal that you do. The first is to reduce your costs and the second is to increase your margin.

Cutting costs

There are two aspects to this. The first is to keep your overhead costs as low as possible. Your overhead costs have to be covered by all of your sales in the year. For example, you might:

→ shop around to save money on things like insurance and not simply renew each year without checking;

→ make your business as green as possible so that your energy consumption is low;

→ hire in specialist equipment only when you need it, rather than buy or lease it and have it as an overhead cost.

You can reduce the costs directly associated with delivering your products and services (these are called variable costs) in many ways. For example, you might:

→ pay less for raw materials;

→ increase your efficiency;

→ buy stock and raw materials only when you need them so that you are not financing stock;

→ contract out your delivery rather than run your own van.

Increasing margin

There is often more scope to increase your profit by making a greater margin on each sale that you make. Here are some examples.

→ Charge for things that you might otherwise give away for free.

- Why not charge for delivery?
- Why not charge to take away and recycle the machine you are replacing?
- Why not agree an ongoing monthly fee to cover maintenance rather than waiting for the client to call you when things break down?

→ Sell extras – in particular, other things that you know your customer will need. Here are some examples.

- A garage offers to valet cars when in for a service at a discount from the usual rate.
- An off-licence sells or hires glasses.
- A carpet cleaning contractor offers to organise curtain cleaning as well and subcontracts the work to a local laundry.

Make a list of the other things that your customers will buy at the same time as they are buying from you. Work out how you can supply those, too, making life easier for your customers and more profitable for yourself.

Time

One of the biggest pitfalls into which new entrepreneurs tumble is to overlook the cost of their own time. If you are engrossed in what you are doing it is very easy to forget how much time something is taking. If you have started your own business, you will be working long hours – and all of these should be paid for by your customers.

Managing your time, and in particular recording it, is one of the most important things you can do when you start a business. You can buy simple software packages that sit on your PC and log your time against different jobs. Easier, perhaps, is just to write down in your diary each day how many hours you spend on each job. You will be surprised at how much time you are not charging for or are building into the cost of the products or services you are delivering.

Case study

Carol Martin-Sperry, Psychotherapist,
www.shrinkrap.co.uk

Carol was prompted to train to become a psychotherapist by the breakup of a friend's relationship. 'I got involved in trying to talk to them,' she said, but realised she didn't know how to be truly effective in helping them. Six months' training followed and for the past 20 or so years Carol has worked with both individuals and couples from her home in West London.

She sees most of her clients for just under an hour a week and believes the most she can work with at any one time is 20. That's not to say she works just 20 hours a week. Carol also has fortnightly supervision sessions and needs time to read, research and maintain her own well-being.

Carol charges up to £100 per session so that she can make a living and maintain the all-important balance between her professional and private lives.

Top Tip

If you are selling your time, either as a consultant or delivering a service, assume that you will sell only three days per week of your time. The rest will be taken up by administration, marketing, cancellations and 'stuff'. 'Stuff' is an all-embracing term to cover those things you did not plan to do but found you had to do anyway!

Frequently asked questions

The following are some questions that entrepreneurs have asked about how to increase profits.

It's all very well saying sell to bigger customers, but I have a retail shop in a fairly hard-up town. How can I go upmarket and make more money?

I guess one thing you could do is to market yourself to more affluent people living a little further away. The appeal to them could be that you are cheaper than the trendier outlets they are accustomed to shopping in. The other option is to look for more and more budget brands that you can sell at an affordable price and on which you can still make a decent margin.

We are running a social enterprise and want to make a difference, not a profit. What does all this mean to us?

Please do not think that a social enterprise is not about profit. What sets you apart from the for-profit business is that you are choosing to invest your profits in helping people over some particular disadvantage. Everything here about increasing your profit applies equally to a social enterprise.

We are a wholesale tree grower. Our customers are garden centres. How can we add value? I'm struggling to see the opportunity for us.

Every business has the opportunity to add value and increase its margins in some way. One obvious opportunity is to develop a retail brand and sell direct to people with large gardens via the internet. They will pay for delivery and you would save the garden centre's margin. You might use a different trading name for this so that you do not end up competing with your garden centre customers.

While it will be very satisfying to watch your business expand, that growth will bring with it some additional things to watch for, as you'll discover in the next chapter.

Key points

→ It takes no longer to win a large order than it does to win a small one.

→ The more difference your product or service makes, the higher your profit from that transaction can and should be.

→ Reducing your costs can increase your profits by more than increasing your price.

→ Do not overlook the time it takes you to do what you do. Your time has to be paid for somehow.

Next step

It's human nature to want your business to be big and well-known, but, before you plan to grow your turnover, remember the old adage: 'Turnover is vanity, profit sanity.' It's profit that you take home and spend!

_____

_____

_____

_____

Financial factors to watch as you start to grow

Chapter Twenty-two

Watching your business grow and evolve will be one of the most satisfying things you do over the coming years. It's like raising a child. What right now might be little more than an idea on a piece of paper will develop into a thriving enterprise, perhaps even a household name.

You have already read about the importance of accurate bookkeeping and also some ways to make your profits bigger. Now it is time to take a closer look at some of the financial implications of business growth.

It is a fact that more businesses fail when they are growing than when they are shrinking. This is because they simply run out of money. However, growing your business is something you do not want to avoid, because standing still is really not an option.

This chapter will help you ride the wave of business growth.

 Be not afraid of growing slowly; be afraid only of standing still. CHINESE PROVERB

Why every business should seek growth

Nothing in life or business ever stays the same. In many ways a business is like a person. It is born, grows, matures, grows old and then moves on in some way. The serial entrepreneur knows this. They grow a business to the point at which they think it will achieve the best sale price and then sell and start again. Others keep their business to the point beyond which it has value and are forced to close it down.

Whatever your ambition for your business, it will evolve and grow because you will constantly need new customers to replace those that fall away. Both you and your new customers will have different expectations, as you will be more experienced and they will be buying from a more established business.

What you can do and, indeed, should do is to manage the rate of growth to keep business evolving in line with your own ambition.

You will either step forward into growth or you will step back into safety. ABRAHAM MASLOW

What is solvency and how does it change?

A business is solvent when it can pay its current business debts as they become due. It is insolvent if it cannot pay its debts or if the assets of the business are less than the debts.

As a business grows, often there is a lag between the growth in costs and the increased income resulting from those costs. In other words, even though you have lots of orders, you have to buy the materials and hire people to fulfil those orders before seeing the income from this additional work. If you have to pay for supplies before you see the income from customers your cash flow is squeezed. This is sometimes called 'overtrading'.

An example would be a company that buys timber and sells shelves to a DIY shop, which then sells them on to the general public. The timber supplier demands payment within 30 days of supply and the DIY shop pays the company at the end of the month following supply.

The wholesale price for which the company sells its shelves to the DIY shop is exactly twice the price it pays for its timber. In other words, it takes £500 worth of timber to make £1,000 worth of shelves.

The shelves are proving popular and orders are growing. The DIY shop orders ahead like this:

	Month 1	Month 2	Month 3	Month 4
Orders placed	£1,000	£2,000	£4,000	£6,000

Here is the impact on the books of the company that makes the shelves:

	Month 1	Month 2	Month 3	Month 4
Opening bank balance	£500	£0	£0	£0
Purchases	£500	£1,000	£2,000	£3,000
Income	£0	£1,000	£2,000	£4,000
Closing bank balance	£0	£0	£0	£1,000

You can see that, even though orders are growing healthily, the company runs out of money very quickly. In this example, that would not be a problem if the company had agreed an overdraft with its bank.

Often this cash flow gap is exacerbated by the need to hire additional staff or buy more or bigger equipment. These add to the costs and inevitably have to be paid for, at least in part, before the sales revenue starts to build.

> ### Top Tip
>
> Do not commit yourself to significant additional fixed costs, particularly permanent labour, until you are confident that sales growth is sustainable. If you are experiencing a temporary increase in demand, hire in the equipment you need and use agency staff.

How to manage this aspect of growth

The big issue here is that you do not necessarily have the money to cover your growing costs until your customers pay you. You can manage this funding gap by:

→ negotiating longer payment terms with your suppliers;

→ persuading your customers to pay you faster (perhaps offering a small discount for paying early);

→ forecasting your cash flow and obtaining an overdraft from your bank to fund the gap;

→ increasing your prices to keep a greater margin and perhaps limit growth resulting from being too cheap;

→ finding an investor in your business (see Chapter Nine).

Paying late and getting paid early is a good way to boost your working capital. Only do this by negotiation, though!

Case study

Warren Bennett, A Suit That Fits,
www.asuitthatfits.com

Former schoolfriends Warren Bennett and David Hathiramani set up A Suit That
Fits in 2005 when they were both 24. Warren had just come back from doing
voluntary work in Nepal where a tailor had made him a hand-tailored woollen suit.

On returning to the UK, Warren wore his suit when he met with David.
They were so impressed with the craftsmanship that they decided to use their
respective engineering and IT backgrounds to simplify tailoring. Their mission was
to enable everyone to quite literally be able to buy a suit that fits! They started
trading from Hampstead market and used their credit cards to fund a small studio
close to Liverpool Street Station.

Word soon spread and the business has grown rapidly. Soon, Warren and
David had a network of ten studios around the UK and a team of style advisers
to operate them. Demand continued to grow but, rather than invest in more
permanent studios, they created pop-up TailorStops.

To operate the TailorStops, style advisers travel around the country setting
up temporary studios in 24 additional towns and cities. Customers can book an
appointment online and enjoy the convenience this local service provides. Warren
and David have enabled their business to keep growing without running out of cash.

What will your bank manager look out for
and why?

Your bank manager will be keeping an eye on the transactions going
through your account. The banks have software that uses your bank
statement to analyse your business performance. These systems will
alert your bank manager to any growing problem.

You must also keep an eye on some key financial ratios within your
business as they can give you early warning of any looming challenge.

These include the following.

Acid test

Acid test is a ratio that shows if a company is able to pay its debts. This is the equation:

$$\text{Acid test} = \frac{\text{current assets} - \text{stock}}{\text{current liabilities}}$$

A score of greater than one passes the test. In fact, the higher the number, the better. Less than one and you are probably insolvent.

Debtor days

Debtor days is a ratio that tells you how many days on average your debtors (people who owe you money) are taking to pay. This is the equation:

$$\text{Debtor days} = \frac{\text{trade debtors}}{\text{annual sales}} \times 365$$

The lower the number the better.

Creditor days

Creditor days is a ratio that tells you how many days on average you are taking to pay your trade creditors (people to whom you owe money). This is the equation:

$$\text{Creditor days} = \frac{\text{trade creditors}}{\text{annual purchases}} \times 365$$

The equations in action

Here's an example to help you fully understand these equations. Management accounts show that, today, your company:

→ is owed £15,000;

→ owes £2,500 to suppliers, £2,000 in wages at the end of the month and £1,000 rent and rates;

→ has stock in the warehouse that cost £3,000;

→ spends £25,000 a year with suppliers;

→ has annual sales of £100,000;

→ has £2,000 in the bank.

Using these figures, we come up with the following results:

$$\text{Acid test} = \frac{\text{current assets} - \text{stock}}{\text{current liabilities}} = \frac{(£15,000 + £2,000) - £3,000}{£2,500 + £2,000 + £1,000} = 2.5$$

The company is very healthy and able to meet its commitments.

$$\text{Debtor days} = \frac{\text{trade debtors}}{\text{annual sales}} \times 365 = \frac{£15,000}{£100,000} \times 365 = 54.75 \text{ days}$$

The company's customers on average pay their invoices in 54.75 days.

$$\text{Creditor days} = \frac{\text{trade creditors}}{\text{annual purchases}} \times 365 = \frac{£2,500}{£25,000} \times 365 = 36.5 \text{ days}$$

The company on average pays its suppliers in 36.5 days.

This company is clearly in good health financially.

Top Tip

If you find yourself stalling creditors because there's not enough money in the bank your business might be less profitable than you think. Don't kid yourself that stretching cash flow is a sustainable tactic.

When are these things most important?

It is always important to keep an eye on some of these key financial ratios, but more so when your business is growing rapidly. Paradoxically, it is when you are growing fast that you are at greatest risk of running out of money. This is also a period when you have very little spare time and it is easy to overlook financial management.

Lifestyle	High growth
Even if your business is a part-time venture, perhaps to supplement a pension, you need to take financial management seriously. Otherwise your business could become an expensive hobby!	Rapid growth is the most dangerous time for business cash flow. When you're seeing sales rocket, watch these key financial ratios carefully. If you start to see worrying trends developing, act immediately!

Other financial things to keep an eye on

There are several other financial indicators that it is wise to monitor. Some relate to your business and others relate to your customers and even competitors. Your own performance is of paramount importance to you, but this often means more when compared with the performance of others.

The following points are not exhaustive, so use them to stimulate your thinking and build your own list. Remember that it is better to start by measuring too many things and then relax than to do it the other way round.

→ **Bank balance** If you manage your cash flow well and have a sound business, your bank balance could at times be substantial. Most banks offering business banking will help you to set up a deposit account into which you can easily switch cash that is not needed immediately. Not only will this earn a modest rate of interest but it will also help you discipline yourself to put money aside for tax and VAT.

→ **Credit limits** If you use a sophisticated bookkeeping package, it will allow you to set credit limits for customers and warn you if you exceed them. Your credit cards have credit limits that prevent you from borrowing more than the card company feels appropriate – you should do the same with your customers.

→ **Overdue debtors** The simplest way to keep track of this is to file copies of invoices raised in date order, with the oldest at the front. Every week, go through the file and chase for payment those that are overdue. Make notes on the copy invoices to remind you of progress.

→ **Competitor accounts** If your rivals are limited companies, they must file accounts with Companies House. There are a number of online databases you can subscribe to, as well as being able to order copies of their accounts from Companies House. These will help you see how your rivals are prospering (you can download any registered charity's most recent accounts free of charge from the Charity Commission website). However, if a limited company is below a certain turnover threshold, you will not be able to find their turnover and profit figures. Only companies above a certain size have to make full accounts public.

Case study
Karin Hermans, Wood You Like,
www.woodyoulike.co.uk

Karin co-owns Wood You Like, a Kent-based supplier and installer of natural wooden flooring. She has linked together online bookkeeping, e-commerce and CRM software to make her business' back office efficient.

Cleverly, she has also set up systems so that she receives email prompts when tasks need doing or some of the performance ratios change. This means she can focus on running her business, confident that behind the scenes her back office software will tip her off when her attention is needed.

Frequently asked questions

Here are some questions that new entrepreneurs have raised regarding financial matters and business growth.

I'm semi-retired, have a pension and only want my business to pay for extras and keep my mind active. Why would I want to seek growth?
It is a fact of life that if a business is not growing, it's probably slipping behind. Growth, however, is relative to personal aspiration. Imagine yourself in a canoe, paddling upstream on a river. If you like the view where you are, you only need to paddle hard enough to maintain your current position.

I've checked my debtor days and now realise why I'm always feeling hard up. People are taking ages to pay me! What can I do to get the money in sooner?
Here are five ways to ensure that you're paid faster.

1 Take deposits and money up front from customers.

2 Invoice for payment in 14 rather than 28 days. It'll seem overdue sooner.

3 Make a courtesy call to your customer when the invoice is due, to check that all is well and that the invoice is in the next payment run.

4 Don't be embarrassed to ask for the money if it's late.

5 Take payment by instalments if your customer appears hard up and is waiting until they can pay the bill in full.

As a very small new business, it seems pretentious to set credit limits for my customers. What will they think?
In short, they needn't know. Credit limits are no more than your way of making sure you don't get too exposed to the risk of bad debt with one customer. You don't tell the customer there's a limit; you just tell them you're owed too much to continue supplying and 'need a cheque now, please' if they go over the limit.

If you want to delve even more deeply into growing your business, see *How to Grow Your Business for Entrepreneurs* by Alex Blyth (Prentice Hall Business, 2009). Naturally, starting and growing a business entails some risk. In the next chapter you'll learn how to minimise risk and increase your chances of success.

Key points

→ Every business needs to grow, even to stand still.

→ Watch the key financial ratios.

→ Set credit limits for regular customers to minimise your risk.

→ If you think you're becoming insolvent, seek professional help. Often if you act quickly enough, the decline can be reversed.

Next step

Take a look again at your business and decide which are the most critical performance indicators. Set things up so you can easily see 'up to the minute' how these are doing. Don't try to measure everything, just what matters most.

_____

_____

_____

_____

How to minimise risk and sleep well at night

Chapter Twenty-three

Nothing we do in life is without risk. When we work for someone else, our employer makes sure our workplace is safe and that we are adequately trained for the job. They also bear the financial risks that go with the business they're in. Even in the public sector there is the very real risk of budget cuts and policy changes.

Now you're becoming an entrepreneur, you are suddenly taking responsibility for risk. It can be daunting to find yourself responsible for things that in the past would have been taken care of by somebody else. Now you alone make the decisions and you alone carry the can if things go wrong.

The skill of managing risk is to keep it in perspective. The media will always remind you that at times people encounter the most horrific disasters and calamities. Most who start a business never experience any major problems. That's because they take care to manage and thus minimise the risk to themselves, those around them and, perhaps most importantly, their livelihood.

 Every business and every product has risks. You can't get around it. LEE IACOCCA

What risks do you face when you start a business?

The most obvious risk you face when you start a business is financial. You are risking your money and perhaps also that of family and friends. You may also be giving up the security of a monthly pay cheque. You can manage financial risk by following the advice contained in the earlier chapters of this book. Working to a business plan, monitoring your financial performance and making sure you are paid on time will minimise the risk of financial disaster.

However, there are some other risks you need to be aware of.

How to Start Your Own Business for Entrepreneurs

Your health

Starting a business can be physically exhausting. However carefully you plan, you will find yourself working long hours. It is also very difficult to take time off sick and, when you are leading a very small team, it is far harder to take the odd week off, as you may have done in a former life.

If you have started your business specifically to trade life in the office for working outdoors, your health may dramatically improve. For others who find themselves compelled to work long hours with few breaks, health might suffer. To look after your health as you develop your business:

→ make sure you take time out for meals and eat sensibly;

→ find time in your life for exercise, even if it is just walking the dog.

Your peace of mind

We all fear the unknown – and starting a business for the first time can be frightening. It is not unusual for new business owners to worry about their enterprise. Indeed, some anxiety is good because it focuses the mind and spurs us on. Too much stress, however, can be damaging. For your own peace of mind, think about:

→ regular reality checks, comparing business performance against business goals, to help you keep things in perspective;

→ maintaining balance in your life so that your business does not occupy every waking moment.

Top Tip

It will help you keep your business challenges in perspective if you also set some personal goals and work to achieve them. Make them realistic and ideally involve physical exercise!

Your relationships

Your preoccupation with your new business is important, but will your life partner, and any children you have, feel left out? Some partners describe a new business as a mistress, taking the person they love away from them. Do not lose sight of the need to spend time with your significant others. Remember that there are few business disasters as expensive as a divorce.

Case study

Craig Dearden Phillips, Stepping Out Ltd,
http://stepping-out.biz

Craig stepped down as CEO of the successful social enterprise he'd grown from scratch to start again in a new venture. Stepping Out was founded in 2010 and helps public-sector organisations, teams and individuals 'step out' from the public sector to create their own organisations. Now in its second year, Stepping Out is already recognised as one of the leading players in its field.

An experienced entrepreneur, Craig knows that it's important to keep work challenges in perspective. He finds that competitive running helps and forces him to make the time to train for the two half-marathons he runs each year. He says some of his best work ideas come to him when running.

Red tape and how to avoid getting it wrapped round your neck

Bureaucracy in all its shapes and forms can appear to be a minefield when you start a business. There are literally thousands of regulations, rules and legal obligations that have the potential to impact your success.

By following a few simple rules of your own, you will manage to keep red tape in check and not find yourself drawn into a morass of regulatory paperwork. The fact is that some regulations are more important than others and not everything will apply to your business. Ask yourself the following questions.

Am I at risk of breaking the law?

In general, the law relating to you as an entrepreneur is the same as the law relating to you as a citizen. The difference is that, as an entrepreneur, you have more opportunity to break the law and to do it on a greater scale. Do not be tempted by illegality in any shape or form.

As an entrepreneur you are legally responsible for the things that your business and, particularly, any employee does. In other words, if your employee is injured at work, you will be considered at fault. The same applies if a customer is injured by a faulty product. You can get more information about this by talking to:

→ an insurance broker specialising in business insurance;
→ membership organisations that represent small businesses – for example, the Federation of Small Businesses (**www.fsb.org.uk**);
→ trade associations representing businesses in your sector.

Am I at risk of losing business?

Your customers are the most important people you have to please. Because the products and services you supply may form an integral part of the products and services your customers, in turn, supply, there will inevitably be legislation with which they will expect you to comply. A good example of this would be the supermarkets, which need documentary evidence that the food products they buy have been transported within a very specific temperature range. Each consignment will be accompanied by a printout from the truck's chiller unit.

Another example is if you supply services to the public sector. They will expect you to have written policies that demonstrate you are up to date with employment, diversity and other legislation. This protects them from criticism by their stakeholders.

You can get more information by talking to:

→ your customers and potential customers;
→ trade associations representing businesses in your sector.

Am I at risk of losing money?

Arguably the biggest risk of losing money, apart from trading, is from incurring uninsured losses. These can occur because:

→ you forgot to insure your car for business use and had an accident on the way to a client;

→ your house was burgled and your office computers are excluded from your household policy;

→ a customer slips and breaks a leg, then sues you and you do not have public liability insurance.

Get more information by reading on.

Insurance – dos and don'ts

Nobody likes buying insurance and one of the truest adages in the business world is that 'no one has endurance like a man who sells insurance'. Insurance is difficult to sell and can be annoying to buy; you only see the value when you have to make a claim.

The insurance that you buy for your business will clearly depend on the business you're in. To find out what you need, talk to a specialist business insurance broker. Alternatively, you can often buy discounted specialist business insurance through trade and membership organisations. These are particularly useful for the kinds of cover the high street brokers rarely arrange – for example, professional indemnity insurance, which you will need if you provide advice in any shape or form.

When buying business insurance, do:

→ make sure you have the basics covered from day one – including public liability, employer liability (if you have employees), vehicle, premises, contents and stock;

→ shop around and talk to more than one broker;

→ negotiate monthly premium payments rather than 12 months in advance;

→ get the 'need to cover' risks covered first and worry about the 'nice to cover' risks later.

Don't:

→ buy insurance to cover more obscure risks without careful consideration – for example, your accountant might suggest you buy insurance that would cover their fees should you be subject to a tax investigation;

→ forget that your bank will probably try to sell you insurance as well – because they will need life cover for security on any borrowing and your bank manager will have a sales target to reach. (You can often negotiate an additional period of free banking when you buy insurance from your bank.)

Top Tip

Remember that people selling you insurance are in business, too. Some will sell you what they know you need. Others will encourage you to buy what they want to sell you. Caveat emptor!

> **There are worse things in life than death. Have you ever spent an evening with an insurance salesman?** WOODY ALLEN

Intellectual property

Many of us dream of inventing or developing something that we can market exclusively and make a lot of money from. If you have created something completely new, you need to protect it from being copied by competitors. You do this by patenting the product.

Patents, trademarks and copyright are very specialist areas. You need expert advice particular to your situation. A good place to start is with the UK government's Intellectual Property Office. Its website at **www.ipo.gov.uk** allows you to search existing patents and contains lots of useful advice.

If you are developing something that you think you might need to protect in the future, you can often get development grants from your regional development agency. You can find out more about these by talking to your local Business Link.

There are two key points to remember about intellectual property (IP). The first is a practical point. You cannot patent something you have told people about. When you speak to a business adviser or patent attorney they will sign a 'non-disclosure' agreement, which means you can discuss it with them.

The second point is more pragmatic. Patenting an invention does not stop someone from copying it. What it does is enable you to take them on in court and stand a very good chance of winning your case. Remember that litigation can be very time-consuming and expensive.

Lifestyle	High growth
If you're not focused on growth, protecting your IP will probably not be a big concern. Perhaps more important is to make sure you're not infringing someone else's IP.	When you come to sell a growing business, buyers will want to know that all IP is protected. In a high-growth business, investment in good IP advice is essential.

Case Study

Mark Collins, Surface Control Ltd, www.surfacecontrol.com

An industrial chemist specialising in flooring, Mark Collins was aware that slippery floors were a huge problem. People slipping over at work, in shops and public buildings is costly, with companies keen to avoid personal accident claims and sick leave.

Mark developed the Slip Guardian, a machine that digitally measures a floor's slipperiness. This, he reckoned, would enable people to monitor risk and plan maintenance more easily.

Aware of the complexity and costs associated with patenting and taking a new invention to market, Mark teamed up with Trevor Baylis Brands. This company, founded by the inventor of the wind-up radio, works with inventors on a shared equity basis. This gave Mark a trusted partner with the expertise and resources to help him capitalise on his invention. See **www.trevorbaylisbrands.com**.

<table>
<tr><td>

Top Tip

If there's no market then there's no point in protecting intellectual property. The value is in its potential.

</td></tr>
</table>

Frequently asked questions

The following are questions that may be raised by new entrepreneurs after reading this book about the risks involved in starting a business.

You say that it is important to protect your health when you start a business, but my health is already poor as I live with a disability. Does this mean I should not start a business?

On the contrary, you should start a business because you have a disability. Creating your own work environment enables you to tailor your work and lifestyle to meet your personal needs. Just because you find some things more difficult than others, so, too, will there be things that you find far easier. Choose a type of business that works for you and enjoy success.

Much of the work I plan to do is commissioned by public-sector organisations. The paperwork they need as part of the prequalification for the tendering process is daunting, to say the least. I am not sure where to start. Where would you begin?

I would begin as a subcontractor to a larger organisation that is already active in this field and working with these organisations. This will enable you to build a reputation with the service commissioners, without having to jump through all the compliance hoops you are describing.

Of course, you will earn less than if you contracted direct, but initially you will probably win more work as a subcontractor than by trying to tender and work direct yourself. You can fill in those forms later, when you are better established and more likely to be successful.

▶

I am something of an inventor and have created what I believe is a world-changing product, which will revolutionise the way people work in my industry. As you say, patenting my product is a long and expensive process. How can I be sure it will be worthwhile?

The answer is simple: you need to research your market. The more evidence you have that your product really is going to revolutionise your industry, the more confidence you will have when it comes to spending money. Don't forget to talk to your regional development agency about development grants to help you take the product to market.

Even if you start out as a one-person business, the time may come when you hire employees. The next chapter will show you how.

Key points

→ Look after yourself as well as your business.

→ Stay legal and buy insurance to cover the most important risks.

→ Protecting your inventions and designs can be expensive. Make sure there is a market first.

Next step

Of all the tips in this chapter the most important is that you look after your own health and well-being. Make a plan right now to include some 'me time' in every working day.

_____

_____

_____

_____

Your first employee – how to take this giant leap

Chapter Twenty-four

Many entrepreneurs will tell you that taking on their first employee was far more difficult than they had imagined. That's not surprising when you realise that what you are doing by employing someone is doubling your workforce.

What's more, as the business founder, you need little management and no motivation from anyone else. You have taken some risks and are looking forward to reaping the rewards. You have developed the mindset of an entrepreneur.

Your first employee is also taking a risk. They are joining a young business to do a job that no employed person has done there before. Both you and the person you hire will want the business to succeed, but at times both of you may find things tense and perhaps even traumatic.

As a new employer, you will be very aware of the cost of your employee. Every minute that they are not hard at work will seem like an hour to you. You will also need to be both their boss and their work colleague at the same time. You will inevitably be working closely together yet must also maintain some distance.

 If you want creative workers, give them enough time to play. JOHN CLEESE

Lifestyle	High growth
Many people intentionally keep their business small enough to manage without hiring staff. There's nothing wrong with doing this. It is your business after all!	Many high-growth businesses start with a team. You might have transferred a department out of a larger organisation. Don't underestimate the impact on each individual of the change of employer from large company to start-up.

When is the right time to hire someone to help?

There is no secret formula for deciding on exactly the right time to become an employer. Every business situation is different and, while some will want to work all the hours there are before 'giving in' and sharing the workload, others will be happy to delegate as soon as possible.

Hiring someone is not for the short term. It is a long-term commitment – financial, contractual and, not least, emotional. Your early employees will be buying into your vision and placing great faith in your ability to maintain and grow the business. That is a great responsibility for you to assume.

Conversely, your employee will put their own interests ahead of yours. They are working for a fixed rate of pay. At times, certainly early on, they might even be earning more than you, but, later, when your investment in their time begins to pay off, they will be very aware that your earnings are growing quickly.

It is probably the right time to take on your first employee when:

→ you are confident the workload will continue to grow;
→ work is profitable enough to justify it;
→ your goal is to continue to grow the business;
→ there are specific tasks and responsibilities that together will make up an interesting and worthwhile job.

Of course, some businesses need staff from day one. For example, if you are running a taxi company you will need taxi drivers. If this is you, then you need to be confident that the work is there for the people you recruit from the very beginning. Starting a business with people on the payroll means:

→ your overhead costs will be higher per month;
→ you will need to have the time to manage effectively both the business and your employees.

Top Tip

Remember that, while you're an entrepreneur, the people who apply for a job with you will simply be looking for a rewarding, stimulating and secure job.

Case study

Brendan Moore, East Anglian Brewers Ltd,
www.eastanglianbrewers.com

Formed in 2002 and now representing more than 40 small East Anglian brewers, the co-operative was for many years run by volunteer members. Chairman Brendan Moore wanted to raise the co-op's game and really put East Anglian beer on the map.

'We had the money but not the time', commented Brendan. He approached the University of East Anglia (UEA), which runs a graduate intern programme. This led to undergraduate Louis Welcomme spending a summer working for the co-operative to put together a business plan with the members.

When Louis returned to university at the end of the summer, the co-operative offered him a job when he graduated. The internship enabled both Louis and the co-op to get to know each other, as well as build the momentum needed to take the organisation forward.

Try before you buy

Before you take on your first employee, it often makes sense to get temporary or short-term help. Such help means you can deal quickly with the heavy workload that confronts you. Recruiting any employee takes time. In fact, if the person you appoint is currently working for someone else, it might be three months between placing your job advert and your new person starting work.

Not only does taking on temporary help get you the support you need faster, but it also gives you the opportunity to experiment a little with the job role and description before you appoint someone full time. There are several ways to find short-term help.

Temps

There are many agencies that provide temporary staff or regular part-time staff. The agencies employ the people they place on what is called a zero hours employment contract. This means they are employed, but there is no commitment to give them any work.

When you need help, you call the agency and they will provide you with people with the right skills and experience to do the job. The agency invoices you and in turn pays the temps. You do not have to be involved with your temporary workers' tax, National Insurance or holiday pay. Nor do you have to worry if the work dries up and you have to let them go.

The agency charges you a higher hourly rate than it pays the worker. For example, let's say you run an events business and need security, bar and waiting staff whenever you have an event to run. Working with an agency means you can hire the staff you need when you need them and, if the people you usually have are not available, the agency will find others.

Consultants

Consultants are freelance workers who will work for you on a project basis. Although you are probably thinking about management consultants, they can be IT specialists, telesales professionals, market researchers, translators or almost anything else you can imagine and might need. Most people working in this way are simply good at their job and prefer the freedom and flexibility of self-employment.

Many people who have taken early retirement and want to stay active in their professional field also work as consultants.

You can find consultants and freelancers by:

→ searching business networks, both online (e.g. **www.ecademy.com**) and offline (e.g. Chambers of Commerce);

→ posting projects on specialist online freelancer websites, such as **www.peopleperhour.com** and **www.skillfair.co.uk**;

→ asking people you know to recommend someone.

> ### Top Tip
>
> Before looking for freelance help, write a very specific project brief that details what has to be achieved. That way you can brief the freelancer properly and, more importantly, measure the success of the project.

What's involved in becoming a boss?

Being a boss means achieving things through other people's efforts and activities rather than your own. The single biggest challenge you face is to let go and delegate things that you have been doing yourself up to now.

In fact, of all the skills you need as a manager of people, the ability to delegate is perhaps the hardest to acquire. You want your employee to do a good job and have hired them to do just that, but do not underestimate how difficult it is to stand by and watch them do something you know you could do better and faster yourself.

Apart from delegating, or learning to delegate, there is much more involved in becoming a boss. You will also have the following responsibilities.

→ Making sure that the workplace is safe and complies in all respects with health and safety legislation.

→ Providing training and support to make sure that your workers are efficient and effective. This means knowing what skills are needed and assessing people's competencies and working with them to plug any gaps.

→ Having the cash flow to pay workers on time and also the associated tax and National Insurance.

→ Making sure you have time to manage your team. No longer can you become totally immersed in your work; you now have to supervise the work of others, too.

 ## Don't keep a dog and bark yourself.

SIXTEENTH-CENTURY ENGLISH PROVERB

How to recruit and get it right first time

Although most people have been hired and perhaps promoted in the course of their lives, it is often only when you start your own business that you find yourself recruiting and appointing others.

You will find that, however many job interviews you have attended as a candidate, being the employer in that situation is very different. There are some steps you can follow to get it right first time.

Define the job

First, you have to define the job. It needs a job title and a purpose. Work out what it is that you need done. Ask others who know you and your business well what they think the job should entail. Note that this gets easier the bigger your team becomes.

Benchmark it against others

Next, compare the job with others. Look at similar positions in other businesses. See how the job is described and how much others are paying for the same skills. Don't be afraid to look outside your particular industry. Get a feel for the scale of the job and its impact. Finally, work out how much you think the person will cost and what return on that investment you will get.

Write a job description and person specification

The job description is your opportunity to list the various responsibilities the new person will have. Look at other job descriptions to see how to present yours. Most have a list of basic accountabilities and then make clear that the person will also be responsible for anything else they are reasonably asked to undertake.

You will describe the experience, knowledge and skills you are looking for. Remember that, when recruiting, you can legally base your choice of candidate only on the person's suitability for the job. You cannot select on grounds of age, gender, race, sexual orientation and so on.

Decide how to recruit

There are various ways you can find people interested in working for you. Each is summarised below and each has its strengths and weaknesses. The route, or combination of routes, you choose will depend on your specific situation.

Advertising

Most newspapers and trade magazines carry recruitment advertising. This is the most open way to recruit and will enable anyone looking for a job to find you easily. The most successful recruitment ads are clear, honest, realistic and state the salary range for the job.

Agency

Agencies will have candidates on their books who are looking for a job and will also advertise. An agency can be good if you do not want others to know that you are recruiting. Often an agency will also shortlist, saving you the trouble of doing it yourself. Agencies earn their money by charging a percentage of the first year's salary as a fee. Initially this can be expensive, but, compared with the cost of advertising and your time in shortlisting, an agency can work out cheaper. Agencies also have more experience of recruitment and will be able to advise you about the job itself.

Networking

There is nothing wrong with adding to your interview shortlist someone you have met through someone you know. However, recruiting by networking is rarely the best way to find the right person for the job

How to Start Your Own Business for Entrepreneurs

if you are only looking for one or two people. For highly specialised jobs where there are few people with the necessary skills, though, networking can work well.

Poaching

It is not unusual for people to poach staff from rival firms. This happens a lot in sales teams, where the individual's customer list can seem very attractive. Poaching can lead to disappointment as you never really know how a marketplace will respond to your taking someone from a competitor. Remember that it is important your company is different from your rivals.

At last, Mr Grimsley felt he'd found the supervisor who would instil discipline into his staff.

Interview

When you interview people it is important that you cover all the points relevant to the job. The job description can be a useful document to use to steer the conversation. Use plenty of open questions to get each candidate talking about themselves and what they think they can contribute to your business' success.

If you are not an experienced interviewer and have someone connected with the business (even as an adviser) who can interview alongside you, ask them to do so. Two heads are always better than one in an interview situation and you will find it useful to observe and think while your colleague is interviewing.

Work out the key questions you want to ask before the interview and ask each candidate the same questions. Make the interview as relaxed as possible. People do not perform at their best when feeling pressured (and that goes for you as well as the candidates).

If you work from home, it is worth hiring a hotel room in which to conduct your interviews. It will appear more professional if you interview in a neutral environment.

Offer

If one of the people you interview is, in your view, ideal for the job, you will want to make them an offer. Most jobs are offered on the basis of three months' probation. In other words, you have the option after three months to part company or make their appointment permanent. Remember that it is as much your responsibility as your employee's to make it work.

The best way to offer someone a job is as follows.

→ Conduct a second interview with the most likely one or two people and, at that interview, discuss salary, training and some of the other practical aspects of the job.

→ Telephone your chosen candidate to ask whether or not they will accept the job if it is offered. Congratulate them and thank them for their enthusiasm so far. Discuss starting dates and offer support if they have to resign from their current job. Follow up with a letter confirming your offer. You can find examples of job offer letters on business support websites.

→ Make the offer conditional on satisfactory references, if you feel that would be helpful. Referees have a legal obligation to tell you the truth, but it is unlikely you will learn much from references that you have not already worked out yourself in getting to know the person.

Top Tip

Don't simply hire the best of the bunch because you are desperate to find someone. Use temporary staff to plug gaps and only hire when you find the right person.

The first day

When your new employee joins you on their first day in your company, you have just one chance to make the right first impression. It is the small things that will make the biggest difference. Make sure you have prepared and tidied the area where the new person will work. Make them feel welcome and have enough time set aside to take them through a proper induction into your business and their new job.

Discuss and agree with them on their first day a proper induction programme. List the things that you need to tell them, show them and do. Work through the list with them and add to it things that they might suggest you have overlooked. Make sure you introduce them to people they will meet and need to know – for example, colleagues and key suppliers.

Top Tip

It is important to be friendly to your employees but never become close friends. You need to maintain a professional distance so that you can remain objective.

Frequently asked questions

The following are some of the questions that new entrepreneurs might raise regarding hiring employees.

I like the idea of using freelance staff rather than employing people. Then I can hire and fire as I need and never have more people around the place than I require. Why would I want to employ someone on a permanent basis?
For one thing, how will you maintain quality with a high turnover of people working in your company? If you show no commitment to them, why should they show you commitment in return? A better policy might be to have some permanent staff and then use temps and freelancers at times of peak demand. You can then make your permanent staff responsible for supervising the temps.

▶

I have worked on my own now for three years and am pretty open and friendly. I'm not sure how employing someone and keeping things to myself will work. Perhaps employing people is not for me. What do you think?

Employing your first member of staff is probably the biggest challenge you have faced so far or will face for some time to come. It is the very conundrum you describe that stops businesses growing. Without hiring staff you can only do the work you can do yourself. It might be that you will be happier on your own than with a team. Only you know the answer to that question.

You haven't mentioned recruitment websites such as Monster.com. Do you think they can be effective?

It all depends on what you are looking for and where in the country you are. There is no harm in trying online recruitment websites as well as other media.

Managing employees will be just one of your day-to-day responsibilities. The next chapter explores some others and shows you how to handle them as effectively as possible.

Key point

→ Work out what you really want before you start recruiting.

→ Consider using freelancers/temps initially to fine-tune the role.

→ Don't look for people like yourself. Look for people whose skills and experience complement your own.

→ If you're daunted by the thought of interviewing, find someone more experienced to help. Explain who they are to the candidates.

→ Once you've offered someone a job, you must follow through and deliver what you have promised.

Next step

Hiring your first employee is a major step. Look again at how you've prepared for this and then, when you're certain, go for it. Do be sure to find someone you trust to interview with you.

_____

_____

_____

_____

Growing your business

Measuring what matters

Chapter Twenty-five

When you start a business everything is rather hand to mouth. You have a plan, but somehow things don't quite happen as you expected. Then, as time goes by, things start to change. Your enterprise gathers momentum and becomes far more predictable. Your business is beginning to grow.

As an enterprise grows, it becomes more difficult to remember everything in your head. You need to develop systems; you need to start measuring what matters.

If you've come from a management background, you'll be familiar with 'key performance indicators'. If not, then this section will explain what they are and why they are so important.

> **Management by objectives works if you first think through your objectives. Ninety per cent of the time you haven't.** PETER DRUCKER

Key performance indicators and how to use them

It's rather like those machines they plug you into in hospital that measure your pulse, blood pressure and other important indicators of health. If something starts to go wrong they beep loudly so that help can be summoned quickly.

Key performance indicators are the business equivalent of these machines. You may remember I introduced them in Chapter One. They enable you to keep an eye on the most important ratios and statistics that chart the health of your business. In large organisations, these statistics are often presented visually, as a 'dashboard' on the company intranet.

The starting point for defining these is your business plan. It will state the activities that you're going to undertake for which you will be paid. Your cash flow forecast should predict the flow of money in and out of the business month by month. Together they contain performance figures that you expect to achieve and therefore need to monitor.

For example, imagine that you have a business offering flights in a hot air balloon. The business is seasonal and you charge per passenger, with a minimum charge for three or fewer in the basket. Key performance indicators to watch in this situation might include:

→ the number of flights per month;

→ the average number of passengers per flight;

→ customer satisfaction;

→ the ratio of enquiries to bookings;

→ how much money you are owed;

→ the maintenance schedule for your balloon and equipment;

→ employee efficiency and performance.

By regularly recording your firm's performance against each of these key performance indicators, comparing the actual figure with the target, you can quickly see where you are exceeding your business plan forecast or falling behind it. That is the secret of effective management.

Things to measure and things that measure themselves

Every business is different and so will need to monitor different performance indicators. Some you will need to measure, recording what happens and then using a spreadsheet to compare performance against target. Others, like your bank balance, measure themselves, but you still need to monitor them and compare them with your plan. Finally, some you will measure yourself and others you might well delegate to someone else – for example, your bookkeeper. The key performance indicators for your business might include the following.

Money

Everyone monitors their bank balance. From Chapter Twenty-two you know to keep an eye on creditor and debtor days as well. Another indicator you might watch is the extent to which your customers are paying by credit card as opposed to cheque. With credit cards you pay the card company a small commission but have the money in your bank account immediately. As your business grows, you might find it beneficial to encourage more of your customers to pay by credit card to keep your overdraft within the limit. Because you are measuring what is happening, you have the opportunity to influence it.

Customers

Categorising your customers and measuring the spend per customer in each category enables you to work out who your best customers are. For example, if you run a restaurant you might find that business diners spend more freely than young couples out on a date. Because you are measuring this, you know to adjust your marketing to focus more on recruiting business customers than young couples.

If you sell business to business, you will inevitably have a sales pipeline. This contains the people with whom you are building a relationship that have yet to convert to customers. It might take 100 sales enquiries to generate 50 proposals, of which only 20 turn into firm orders. By monitoring these ratios you know the number of enquiries you need to create one sale and you can also work to improve the conversion rates.

Processes

If you operate business premises, particularly if you make things, you will want to monitor the efficiency of your production processes. Things you might keep an eye on include the physical efficiency of machines, in terms of energy consumption per unit produced. You might also note maintenance and breakdowns so that you can identify where problems are occurring most and deal with the causes.

Finally, you will want to measure your raw material costs and the efficiency with which they are converted into finished products. More expensive raw materials might actually cost less in the long run if they lead to more output and less waste.

People

If you employ people, they will probably form the biggest cost. Without becoming overbearing you want to record their efficiency and performance. In a large organisation sick leave and absenteeism might be important statistics to record. In your organisation you might be more interested in people's productivity and their ability to generate positive customer feedback.

Benchmarking

This could be a topic for a book in itself. Benchmarking is the way to measure your performance against that of others in similar situations. Some trade associations collect key performance indicators (KPIs) from their members and then publish them as a league table. Your competitors are not identified but you can see how your performance compares. Most importantly, benchmarking pushes you to improve your performance because you can see what is possible and has already been achieved by others.

Lifestyle	High growth
Remember that the more effectively you set and measure KPIs the more time you have for other things. No business is too small for KPIs.	In a fast-growing business, it may be worth investing in a bespoke system that measures KPIs and presents them in a readily understandable format. Early on this will seem like a luxury. Later, it'll be an essential.

Case study

Elaine Clark, Cheap Accounting,
www.CheapAccounting.co.uk

Elaine Clark set up Cheap Accounting in 2007. She's been a chartered accountant for more than 20 years. She saw that there was an opportunity to change the way accountants work with small businesses by embracing the internet as part of the accounting practice toolkit.

Her clients input their own transactions via a web portal and this enables Elaine to constantly monitor how they are doing. She is proactive, anticipating client needs and sending email updates and fact sheets.

Most client contact is by email, which enables Elaine to keep her cost base low. Her clients are mostly start-ups and small businesses that welcome an affordable service. By encouraging them to keep their books up to date, she can quickly see where her help is most needed.

Elaine has won the Woman in Finance category of the Network of Aspiring Women Awards in recognition of her work and the business was awarded the title of Progressive Practice in 2010 after a public vote carried out by AccountingWEB and CCH, two very well-respected names in the accounting industry.

Top Tip

Measure what matters most yourself and delegate the rest for others to worry about. Give your people limits of authority, so you can budget effectively.

Delegation and how to do it

The benefits to you of monitoring and adjusting the performance of your business are obvious. The benefits to the people you employ will be less obvious. Unless you involve them in making management decisions, working for you will simply be just another job with hours to work and pay to earn.

As you employ more people, you will need to set them achievable targets so that they know what is expected of them. You should also discuss and agree any training needs necessary for them to develop the skills and efficiency to achieve the targets. The more you involve your employees in making decisions about how their jobs are done, the better motivated they will be to do them.

People who choose to be employees are motivated by different things from people who choose to be employers, but that doesn't mean they will not be willing to accept more responsibility as your business grows. Good ways to delegate to your employees might include:

→ agreeing targets and modest performance bonuses;

→ letting the employees choose when there are two equally productive ways to do something;

→ not judging them by things they cannot influence (it can be easy to blame your staff for things for which you or your customers are responsible);

→ remembering that short-term goals and small rewards are more motivating than long-term goals and large rewards.

Building value into your business

The best reason for building your business is to increase its value. As it gains momentum and you delegate more, it becomes less reliant on you. Freeing yourself from the day-to-day operational affairs makes time for strategic thinking. It also makes your enterprise more valuable to others because it doesn't depend on you for its day-to-day success.

This is the point at which a business takes on a life of its own. It is no longer just you working away on your own or with a small team. Word has spread and the business has a reputation. Customers are starting to come back and encourage their friends and associates to use you as well. All of a sudden things are happening without you having to push them.

When this happens to your business, it is starting to acquire real value. The value in a business is in its future potential and not in what has been done before. The more the business is expected to grow and gain momentum, the more profitable it will be and the more valuable it will become.

If you would be wealthy, think of saving as well as getting. BENJAMIN FRANKLIN

What is a business really worth?

In short, a business is only worth what someone is prepared to pay for it. You can see how businesses are valued in Chapter Seven, which looks at this from the buyer's perspective. Even if you are not considering selling your business, it is worth building in value.

Case study
Simon Campbell, The Sandpit,
http://thesandpit.com

A serial entrepreneur, Simon Campbell was caught running a flea market in the school playground at the age of ten. Eventually, he moved to Spain to work one year for a multinational, liked the country, did not like working for someone so stayed and set up his first three businesses there. He's started, built and sold media, advertising and software companies. His current company, The Sandpit, is a new model for 'sales incubation', investing in technology and providing the sales and marketing team.

I asked Simon how he adds value to his businesses. 'Obviously, the holy grail is to grow the business through sales,' he said. 'Too many companies, especially early stage, spend months trying to raise money where they could have been spending that time selling and generating revenue. Once you do that, raising money is easy and you might find you do not even need it.'

It may sound simple, but having built businesses through fundraising and sales, Simon knows that sales are by far the most important thing.

How to Start Your Own Business for Entrepreneurs

Why is creating value as important as making profit?

The more your business is worth, the more flexibility you have as its owner. Right now, you may not be able to imagine ever wanting to sell it, but one day you might decide that this is the right thing to do. You do not know what the future holds and one of the benefits of having your own business is having as much freedom as possible to live the life that you want to live.

For example, if you are very successful at competing with a large company, they may well decide to make you an offer. That offer might be significantly higher than the open market value of the business. You could at that point decide to sell, put some money away for your retirement and start a new business from a far stronger base.

When will this become an issue for me?

Adding value as well as making a profit is an issue you should be addressing from the day you start your business. Inevitably, in the early months, you will be more concerned with building the enterprise and managing cash flow, but you should always have an eye on the importance of building value as well.

As your business grows, its demand for cash will increase. The faster it grows, the greater that demand will be. The more creditworthy your organisation, the easier it will be to find the money you need to do just that.

Remember, too, that you are in business to make money as well as to make a difference in the marketplace you have chosen to inhabit. It is almost inevitable that, as you develop your business, you will see new opportunities. Sometimes it makes sense to sell what you have and start again, focused on where the greatest opportunity seems to be.

Case study

Simon Wadsworth, The Retail Factory,
www.retailfactory.co.uk

After creating, building and selling several web/digital agencies, it was inevitable that Simon Wadsworth would establish his own e-commerce business. The Retail Factory opened for business in 2007 and plans to be 'the UK's number one online supplier of retail and office supplies'.

Simon sold his earlier companies when approached with a good deal. 'It's difficult to know when it's the right time to sell,' he commented, 'but if the deal looks and feels good, it's probably worth taking.'

Simon also says that the key trick is to put the company in a high-profile position when the buying cycle for your type of company turns to you. 'We always spent a lot of money on marketing and PR,' he told me, 'so that our likely buyers were reading about us all the time.'

How do I add value?

All the way through this book there are examples of ways you can add value to your business. Here is a summary to remind you:

→ make the business less reliant on you by hiring and developing good people;

→ invest constantly in improving your business' capacity to exceed customer expectations;

→ specialise in one aspect of what you do rather than trying to be all things to all people;

→ build customer loyalty so that you can be sure of their continued custom;

→ protect any intellectual property created by your business;

→ maintain a positive public profile and build a good reputation;

→ when your accountant has calculated your annual profit, make sure you leave at least half of it in the business to fund future growth.

Case study

Charlie Stockford, SustainIt Solutions,
www.sustainitsolutions.co.uk

When Charlie Stockford's daughter started at boarding school, she had time to start a new business. A background in both arts and computer software, together with a passion for corporate social responsibility (CSR), led to the creation of SustainIt Solutions.

The business employs eight full time, plus associates, and helps large corporate clients evaluate their return on investment in CSR. Clients include travel, food and IT companies, along with others striving to improve public perception of their products and services while reducing their operating costs.

Charlie's work has enabled her to see that increasingly CSR is an opportunity for small companies, too. In 2009 she rebranded the business and developed a new web-based service that enables even the smallest company to appreciate and measure how important CSR can be for them.

Frequently asked questions

Here are some of the questions that new entrepreneurs ask about the day-to-day operation of their businesses.

I'm a one-man band and fly my business by the seat of my pants. Why should I bother with setting and monitoring targets?

I can think of two good reasons. The first is that if, for example, you break a leg and have to hire someone in to do the work, how will you measure it? The second is that you will surely become more proud of your business if you measure its performance and perhaps benchmark against others.

We are setting key performance indicators and are surprised to find that what we thought of as extras are actually where we make a profit. How can we change this to make a profit on everything we do?

Well, maybe you can't. Maybe, like some of the budget airlines, you will not make your money from the core activity but from all the peripheral products and services ▶

you can sell to your customers on the back of it. What's important is that you don't do things you don't need to do and you make a profit from the whole business.

I'm confused. Surely it's better to have a high income for many years than a lower income and business with a value?
If you run your business properly you will have both. It is for you and your financial advisers to decide what is right for you, your business and your situation. Remember that the sale of business assets is taxed differently from your income from the business. This is particularly relevant when you get to retirement. In general, I would argue that a business with a high value will also give you a good living and an easy life.

Key points

→ Measure the things that matter to your business.
→ Learning to delegate will help you become more strategic.
→ It is never too soon to start to add value to the business.

Next step

Remember that the more your business can operate without you, the more valuable it will become. Once you really have this organised, you can begin to step back from day-to-day operations and think more strategically.

_____

_____

_____

_____

Lifestyle or wealth – a chance to reflect and review your goals

Chapter Twenty-six

As you have worked through these pages, you will have become far more confident in your ability to start and build a successful enterprise. Perhaps you have started your business already and have used this book to fill any gaps in your knowledge or cope with the inevitable challenges as they arise.

It is also highly likely that your plans have changed. In fact, as you continue to grow and develop your new business, you will find your plans constantly evolving. This is because the business landscape itself is constantly adapting and changing, forcing you to adapt and change as well. Some see this as a threat, but it is a huge opportunity.

This final chapter is here to encourage you to constantly scan the horizon for what is new. It is also written to encourage you to reflect on your personal goals as they change over time, so that your business can deliver them to you. In the final analysis, we all start a business to take control of our lives and maintaining that control is crucially important.

> **Only put off until tomorrow what you are willing to die having left undone.** PABLO PICASSO

What have you achieved so far?

Although planning for the future is important, so is recognising what you have achieved to date. It is too easy to forget to enjoy today or celebrate your success so far.

Running a business is rather like learning to ride a bicycle. When you first get on, it seems impossible to balance and make any progress at all. With determination, practice and quite a few bruises, you suddenly master the machine. Soon cycling becomes second nature and you forget how difficult it was in the beginning. Business is just the same.

Once you become confident that your business is on track, you can perhaps begin to look at the bigger picture.

Case study

Andrew Seaton, Resolve IT Solutions,
www.resolvesolutions.co.uk

Andrew Seaton did work experience in a school as part of his university course. He realised that IT support to this sector was poor and vowed to improve it. He also discovered he had a natural aptitude for IT because he enjoyed solving problems.

On graduating, Andrew soon recruited two schools he knew as his first clients and quickly grew the business from there. Now, four years later, his business is established and profitable. It continues to grow, but not at the expense of quality of service.

Andrew has also learned to manage his own expectations and is determined not to become a slave to his company. As he told me, 'I am very lucky that I enjoy my work and find it rewarding, but it's not the be-all and end-all of life.'

Work/life balance

When you start your business it demands every minute of your time. As it becomes established it remains demanding, but less so than in the early months. This is your opportunity to get your life back in balance.

One of the paradoxes of business is that you have the best ideas when you are not at work. It is important to find time to escape from the day-to-day challenges of your enterprise and reflect on the bigger picture. Your family will also appreciate both your company and the opportunity to contribute to your strategic business planning.

Of course, being an entrepreneur is a way of life, but it is very much up to you to make it the kind of life you would like to lead. Here are some examples of ways to help maintain your work/life balance.

→ **Go on a mini-retreat every few months** This gives you time and space to reflect on your business progress and consider future plans. It could be as simple as a quiet afternoon on the beach with a notebook and pen or as complicated as a weekend in a monastery where enforced solitude prevents you from being distracted.

→ **Take your family away for the weekend** Many leading entrepreneurs pick up their best business ideas on holiday. Simply going somewhere you have never been before and trying things you have never tried before can enable you to see opportunities. Sahar Hashemi, founder of Coffee Republic, wondered why London did not have coffee shops like those she saw in New York. She decided to start her own. You, too, could find inspiration on holiday.

→ **Develop your social life** An active social life helps you keep your business in perspective. Listening to others talk about their lives, work, challenges and opportunities provides a useful balance for what otherwise might become an obsession. Equally, sharing some of your business experiences with others might prompt obvious questions that you have overlooked.

> **Top Tip**
>
> All work and no play will make you less effective. Make time for yourself and your family. Be surprised by how this improves your business creativity.

Longer-term goals

As your business develops over time so, too, will you. Just as it will mature and age so, too, will you. Whatever age you are now you are inevitably going to get older. Your business is the vehicle you will use to meet your changing needs.

This might sound painfully obvious, but think again. If you are in your twenties you will create a very different kind of business from one you will create in your fifties. Your approach to technology, commerce and life itself will be different according to where you are in your life.

As you go through life your priorities will change. Perhaps you are a single parent fitting your business around your childcare, only able to work part time, but knowing that in a few years' time you'll want your business to grow so that when you have time to earn more you can do so. You might be newly retired and simply wanting your business to keep you occupied and supplement your pension. These people would create two very different businesses, potentially in the same marketplace.

In the same way that you have planned your business, there is also merit in planning your life. Writing a life plan can be a very useful and enlightening exercise. Look at your future ambitions and see where you want to end up. Then you can structure and develop a business to make those things a possibility. Almost anything is possible if you put your mind to it. Listen to your instinct or inner voice. If it feels right, it probably is right!

Lifestyle	High growth
In a lifestyle business, your happiness is perhaps the best barometer of success. If you feel good, you'll inevitably be doing OK.	In a high-growth business, you'll probably have sacrificed some time for yourself along the way in your quest to build value. Remember that when you come to sell, you want the right deal, not necessarily the highest price. Put your longer-term needs first!

Frequently asked questions

The following questions reflect some of the concerns entrepreneurs may have regarding the work/life balance highlighted in this book.

I seem to be struggling just to stand still and, at the moment, I cannot envisage a time when it would be different. Why end the book with philosophical stuff about long-term goals? I don't think I'll ever get there.

I think you will get there. There is a lot of truth in Maslow's hierarchy of needs. The scientist found that until your basic needs are met you have no interest in what else might be possible. As you build your business you will become more comfortable and better able to look ahead. This short chapter is here to remind you that, however tough today is, if you've worked at your business effectively, tomorrow will be better. Here is how Maslow pictured the process:

▶

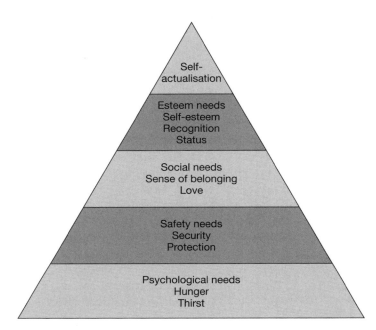

SOURCE: BASED ON A. H. MASLOW (1943), 'A THEORY OF HUMAN MOTIVATION', *PSYCHOLOGICAL REVIEW*, 50(4) 370–96.

You start at the bottom and over time, as each of the needs is met, you see and desire those further up. In business and in life, self-actualisation is the eventual goal.

I have two children and my plan is to create a business that can support them as well as me. I want to build a business that they will inherit and manage. Is that a good idea?

Certainly it is an option, but I would not personally choose to groom my children to take over the family firm. Sometimes it works well and other times it is a disaster. The key seems to be to make sure that your children have wide enough experience of the world of business before they come back to run the family firm. Remember that although you are living the life, you cannot live theirs for them.

Key points

→ Don't overlook what you have accomplished already or forget to celebrate each success as it is achieved.

→ Take time out to reflect on your business and set long-term goals.

→ Acknowledge that, as you age, your personal goals change and your business goals might need to develop to reflect them.

Next step

Make time to compare your goals now with those when you started out. See how your ambition has changed. Keep planning, keep doing and keep winning!

_____

_____

_____

_____

Index

A Suit That Fits 261
accountants
    choosing 56–7, 63, 242–3
    setting up a limited company 61
Accountants Circle, The 123–4
accounts *see* bookkeeping
achievement, recognition of 308
acid test 262
Admiral Design and Print 95–6
advertising
    hiring of employees through 286
    straplines 177
    and websites 193
advisers 118–24
    choosing good 118–19, 126–7
    networks 121–4
    from outside business 120–1
    sharing resources 123
affiliates and websites 194
agencies
    as business type 88
    hiring of employees through 282–3,
        286
    PR (public relations) 207
Aldridge, David 218
alternatives
    in finding right business opportunity
        23–6
    to working from home 69–70
anxiety 271
appearance
    as buying motive 181
    importance to brand 155–6

approach in sales process 214–15
Articles of Association 60–1
assets 240
Avon 45

bad debts 63
bad news 205–6
Baggia, Waqas 98
balance sheet 241
bank account, opening a business
        52, 58–9, 238
bank balance 264, 297
bank managers
    analysis of business performance
        261–2
    and business plans 37–8, 97
bank statements 238
banks
    fees and charges 106
    setting up your business 58–9, 63
    types of 59
Begbie, Julie 81
Bells Play Group 130
benchmarking
    jobs 285
    using key performance indicators
        299
Bennett, Warren 261
BigBarn CIC 111
Blumenthal, Heston 206
BMW cars 152
Bodiam, Ed 119
boilerplate in press release 205

bookkeeping 236–44
   importance of 236–7
   records to be kept 238–9
   software packages 239–40
   on starting business 237–8
boss, becoming a 284
bottom line 241, 247
Bowles, James 56
Bowles Print Management UK 56
brand
   developing 152–61
   key elements 153–6
Branson, (Sir) Richard 67, 224
British Humanist Association 199
brochures, and marketing message
   177
broker as business type 47
Bunday, Craig 121–2
bureaucracy 272–4
business angels 113–14
Business Club 122
business growth
   financial factors 258–67
   importance 266
   measurement 296–306
business idea *see also* business
   opportunity
   market research 30–40
Business Link 126, 174, 276
   website 10, 118, 285
business networks *see* networks
business opportunity *see also*
   business idea
   finding right 18–28
   existing business 81
business performance analysis 261–2
business plans 94–102
   and bank managers 37–8, 97
   contents of good 94–6
   how to write 94, 98–100
   length 96
   professionally written 101
   who needs to read 97–8
business potential 12–13
business premises 66–75
   funding for 105

business rates 61
business structure 52–64
business types 42–9
businesses for sale, finding 82
buying a franchise 45–6
buying an existing business 43, 78–89
   finding 48, 81, 82
   how to buy 84–7
   making an offer 83
   reason for sale 79–80
   versus starting up 78–89
   value 78–9, 84–5
buying motives 180–1, 212–13

Campbell, Simon 302
Carphone Warehouse, The 134
cash flow 241
   managing 106–7, 250, 260, 263
   and solvency 259–60
Cashflow Manager 239
Challis, Steve 179
Chambers of Commerce 62
charities 57–8
Cheap Accounting 300
clarity and consistency, of marketing
   message 179–80
Clark, Elaine 300
Clark, Jeff 95–6
Clarke, Ian 144
closed questions 215–16
Coffee Republic 310
Collins, Mark 276–7
colour, importance to brand 156
commitment
   getting in sales process 216–17,
     218, 221
   getting lasting 219
communication, via marketing
   message 178–9
Community Interest Company (CIC)
   57–8
Companies House 61, 265
competitive people 6, 8
competitors
   accounts 265
   market analysis 36–7
   negative information 183

concentrated marketing message 177
consultants 283
content, on websites 190
content management systems 195
  and websites 190
context of words, for brand
    development 148
convenience, as buying motive 181
Cornwall Cakes 80
Costa Blanca TV 62–3
costs, cutting of 251
credit cards 298
credit extended for funding business
    108
credit limits 264, 266
creditor days 262, 297
creditors 241
CRM (Customer Relationship
    Management) software 220
customers
  exploring needs in sales process
      215–16
  face to face or virtual 144
  finding 142–9, 172
  as key performance indicator 298
  marketplace boundaries 142–4
  need to look beyond the obvious
      145
  paying in advance 108
  public sector organisations 277
  retention 173
  searching for when busy 146
  taking with you 79
  techniques for finding 146–7
  work with in starting a business 132
customers' premises 69, 74
Custwin 191–2

Davidson, Anne 134
Davison, Anthony 111
Dawkins, Richard 199
Dayman, Ben 80
deals
  buying an existing business 86
  levels of profitability 248–9
debtor days 262, 266, 297

debtors 241
  overdue 265
delegation 300–1
determined people 7
direct selling 44–5, 48
Discounter, The 109
Distinctive Weddings 225
distribution, as element of marketing
    168
dividends 243
Domino's Pizza 32
Don't Travel Empty 166–7
due diligence 85, 86–7
Dunstone, Charles 134
durability, as buying motive 181

earn in 86
earn out 86
East Anglian Brewers' co-operative 282
eBay 192, 196, 224
Eccles, Michael 147
economical people 7–8
economy, as buying motive 181
80/20 rule 249
employees 280–90
  and business plans 97
  cost of 285
  first day 289
  hiring of 290
    finding people 286–7
    recruitment 284–8
    temporary or short-term 282–3
    timing 280–1
  managing 284
Ennis, Gary 8–9
Enterprise Finance Guarantee
    Scheme 111–12
entrepreneurs
  setting of goals 9–11
  types of 5–9
  view of opportunities and
      challenges 4, 14–15
equipment, funding for 105
existing business, buying see buying
    an existing business
exit strategy, in business plans 100

expenditure, income and 241
expenses
    funding for living 105
    records to be kept 238
Expresso 32

face-to-face customers 144
Fat Duck, The 206
financial factors, business growth
    258–67
financial indicators other than ratios
    264–5
financial ratios 261–3
    when important 263–4
financial risk 270
first day for new employee 289
focus, importance to brand 153–4
franchise
    business plans 101
    buying a 45–6, 48–9
freelance bookkeeper 236
freelance copywriter 160
freelancers, hiring of 283, 289
funding
    calculating amount needed 104–6
    cash flow forecast 106–7
    where to find 104–15

Garrett, Richard 31
geography as a marketplace
    boundary 143
goals, setting of 9–11
goodwill 227, 228–9
grants, for funding business 111–12,
    115
graphic design 157–9, 160, 161
Greenfinder 21–2
gross margin 241
growth *see* business growth

Hanes, Kate 21–2
Harris, Andy 191–2
Hashemi, Sahar 310
Hathiramani, David 254
headline in press release 203
health risk 271, 277

Hermans, Karin 265
Herne Bay Mobility 218
Hideaways in Hay 147
hiring of employees 290
    finding people 286–7
    recruitment 284–8
    temporary or short-term 282–3
    timing 280–1
HMRC, when starting business 237
holidays 310
home
    working from 66–8, 74
        alternatives 69–70
Hope, John 153
Hope Technical Developments 153
Hotel Indigo 227–8
Hyundai cars 152

image, key elements 153–6
income
    and expenditure 241
    potential 12
income tax 61
increasing margin, for extra
        profitability 252
induction for new employee 289
instinct, and market research 32–3
insurance 237, 275–6
intellectual property 275–7, 278
internet 186–7 *see also* websites
interviewing people 287–8
intuitive people 6–7, 8
investors
    and business plans 97
    for funding business 110–15

jargon 240–1
job benchmarking 285
job definition 285
job description, writing 285–6
job offers 288
journalists
    regard as news 201
    what they are looking for 200

Kashflow 239
Keepstakes 81

key financial ratios 261–3
  when important 263–4
key performance indicators (KPIs) 9,
    296–7, 305–6
  benchmarking 299
  things to measure 296–7
Konectbus 179
Koseoglu, Daniel 5
Kreative Iron 98

landlords, and business plans 97
leases 71–2
legal responsibilities, risk 273
legislation, risk to business 273
liabilities 240
life plan 311
lifestyle, or wealth 308–13
lighting, importance to brand 156
limited company
  business structure 52, 55
  setting up 59, 60–1
LinkedIn 123, 167
living expenses, funding for 105
location of business premises 70–1
long-term goals 10, 310–11
long-term liabilities 240
losses, uninsured 274

Macauley, Ann 130–1
management
  business growth 260
  of cash flow 106–7, 260
  of employees 284
Mannakin 187
Marett, Anthony 166–7
margin, increasing for extra
    profitability 252
market analysis 32, 36–7
market research 30–40
market share, in business plans 99
market size 31, 34–5
market trends 31, 36, 41
marketing 164–74
  funding for 105
  messages 176–84
    best words to use 177–8

beyond words 178–9
buying motives 180–1
clarity and consistency 179–80
concentrated 177
features of a good 176–7
when to use 182
marketplace boundaries 142–4
Martin-Sperry, Carol 253
Maslow's hierarchy of needs 311–12
measurement, of business growth
    296–306
Memorandum of Understanding 60–1
mentors 121, 124–7
Milano, Silvano 70
milestones 10
mini-retreat 309
Mita, Roz 187
mobile business 69
money see also funding
  borrowing through increasing the
      mortgage 108
  funding for borrowing 106
  as key performance indicator 297–8
  risk of losing 274
money-making options, from
    websites 193–4
Monster.com 290
Moore, Brendan 282
Moore, John 135
Morgan, Lesley 227–8
mortgage, increasing for funding
    business 108
motivation
  for selling a business 79–80
  for starting business 30–1
multi-level marketing 44–5
multiple buying motives 181
Murphy, Bláithín O'Reilly 225
My Village News 134

name
  importance to brand 154–5,
      160, 161
  as marketing message 177
National Insurance 236

networks 121
  groups 122
  hiring of employees through 286–7
  marketing to 44–5
  peer support 121
new employee, first day 289
news
  bad 205–6
  as regarded by journalists 201
Nicol, Keith 62–3
NSDesign 8–9

objections, overcoming in sales
      process 217–18
online selling 192–3
online trading 192
open questions 215–16
operating within a separate business
      69, 74
outside advice 120–1
overdue debtors 265
overheads 241
'overtrading' 259

page header in press release 203
page layout, of websites 188–90
Pansophix 144
paperwork, setting up your business
      60–1
paragraphs in press release 203–5
Park 'n' Trim 70
partnership
  business structure 52, 54
  paperwork for setting up 60
party plan 44–5
Patel, Anita 134
Patel, Jayesh 46
patents 275–7, 278
Patterson, Julian 179
PayPal 193, 196
peace of mind risk 271
Peak Electromagnetics 213
peer support 121
people
  in business plans 100
  finding 286–7
  as key performance indicator 299

performance, as buying motive 180
performance-related deals 86
person specification, writing 285–6
personal ambitions and expectations,
      in finding right business
      opportunity 22–3
personal experience, in business
      plans 99
Phillips, Craig Dearden 272
Phone Voice, The 68
photographs 208
  for PR 200, 202
Pitman, Alison 68
Pizza Express 32
place, as element of marketing 168
plans see business plans
poaching, for recruiting people 287
Pocock, Ian 213
PR (public relations) 198–209
  agencies 207
premises see business premises
preparation, in sales process 214
presentation, of solution in sales
      process 216
press releases, for PR 202–5
Price, Martin 154–5
pricing, as element of marketing
      168–71, 173
PRIME (Prince's Initiative for Mature
      Enterprise) 134
Prince's Trust 113, 125, 134
processes, as key performance
      indicator 298
products
  in business plans 99
  as element of marketing 165–7
profit and loss account 241
profitability 246–55
  and adding value 303
  in business plans 100
  calculating 249–50
  how to add extra 251–2
  and turnover 246–7
  and value 248–9
promotion
  as element of marketing 167
  using websites for 188

public relations *see* PR (public relations)
public sector organisations 277

questions, for exploring the customers needs 215–16
QuickBooks software 239

rates, business 61
ratios
   key financial 261–3
   when important 263–4
Ratner, Gerald 224
records to be kept 238–9
recruitment *see* hiring of employees
red tape 272–4
registration agents, setting up a limited company 61
relationships
   with employees 289
   with mentors 125–6
   risk 272
Reliant Packaging 121–2
rent for business premises 72
repeat business 219
reputation 224–31
   building and maintaining 226
   and business value 228–9
   buying an existing business 88
   how good one can work 227
   why important 224–5
research
   market 30–40
   retail locations 73
Resolve IT Solutions 309
Retail Factory, The 304
retail premises 72–3
Rhys-Gill, Karen 45
risk
   in finding right business opportunity 21
   minimising 270–8
   types of 270–4
Robinson, James 109
RSS (Really Simple Syndication) feeds 187
Rubens, Zoë 171

Sage Instant software 239
sales agent as business type, being a 47
sales leads, keeping track 220
sales process 214–18
Sandpit, The 302
Schreiber, Roland 32
Schultz, Howard 78
Seaton, Andrew 309
security, as buying motive 180
self-funding 107–8
selling a business, motivation 79–80
selling online 192–3
selling products and services 212–22
sensitive people 7, 8
services
   in business plans 99
   as element of marketing 165–7
setting of goals 9–11
setting up your business 58–62
sharing resources 123
short-term goals 10
short-term liabilities 240
short-term staff 282–3
signs, as marketing message 177
Signs Express 46
Sinclair, (Sir) Clive 131
Sinsins Lovestore 154–5
SME Advice 119
smell, importance to brand 156
'So what' game 33–4
social enterprise 57–8, 254
social life 310
software packages, for bookkeeping 239–40
sole trader
   business structure 52–4
   paperwork for setting up 60
solvency 259–60
sound, importance to brand 156
SPACED buying motives 180–1, 212
spam, and websites 194
specialist registration agents, setting up a limited company 61
staged purchase 86
Starbucks 78

starting a business
    bookkeeping 237–8
    examples of good timing 134
    motivation 30–1
    timing 130–7
starting from scratch 42, 80–1
starting up see starting from scratch
Stepping Out Ltd 272
stock and materials, funding for 105
Stockford, Charlie 305
straplines 159, 177
stress 271
subscriptions and websites 194
success, in finding right business
    opportunity 19–20
Surface Control Ltd 276–7
SustainIt Solutions 305

taking over existing business see
    buying an existing business
Tania-Tapel 134
tax returns 236–7, 238
taxation
    and bookkeeping 236–7
    setting up your business 61–2
temporary staff 282–3
tenure of business premises 71–2
terminology, used by accountants and
    bank managers 240–1
ThinkDave.Com 182
Tiffin Company, The 5
time
    managing 252–3
    selling 253
timing
    for bookkeeping 241–2
    in finding right business
        opportunity 20
    in starting a business 130–7
Toohey, David 123–4
trading online 192
TUPE (Transfer of Undertakings
    [Protection of Employment]
    Regulations) 87
turnover, and profitability 246–7

Twitter 123
    link on website 190
types of risk 270–4

uninsured losses 274

value
    adding as well as making profit 303
    from business growth 301
    business worth 302
    of an existing business 78–9, 84–5
    how to add 304
    importance of 303
    potential 12–13
    and profitability 248–9
    reputation and business 228–9
    from websites 191
value-added tax 106, 237
    setting up your business 62
video clips 188
virtual customers 144
vision statement 101
    in business plans 98–9
Volvo cars 152

Wadsworth, Simon 304
wealth, or lifestyle 308–13
websites 186–96
    alternative money-making options
        193–4
    benefits of 186–7
    content management systems
        190, 195
    finding customers 148
    page layout 188–90
    for promotion 188
    recruitment 290
    selling online 192–3
    trading online 192
    traffic 195
    value for money 191
White, Jonny 250–1
Wilkinson, David 182
Windcrop 135
Wood You Like 265

words
  best to use for marketing message
    177–8
  techniques in using for brand
    159–60
working from home *see* home,
    working from
work/life balance 309–10
Worth, Jon 199

writing
  business plans 94, 98–100
  person specification 285–6
  press releases 202–5

you word, for brand development 159

Zimma Web Development 250–1